Shijo

Truly Corean
Poetry Cadence Rhymed

Edited by Lee Kyung-hoon

Proofread and Commented by William Edwards

This edition wants to be referred to as ‘Jarng-yoo edition’. ‘Jarng-yoo’ or ‘Jang-yu’ is the place we live in. It is about 30 minutes drive from Busan, the southernmost eastern port city.

Participants

Lee Kyung-hoon : Editor, Preface and Introduction
Seoul National Univ, majored in law
Seoul National Univ, majored in linguistics

Amy Levine : Review
Visiting Professor
Changwon National University

William Edwards : Proofreading, Comments, Reflections
M.A. English & Cultural Studies McMaster University
M. Ed. OISE University of Toronto
Former Visiting Professor Changwon National University

Kim Jin-mook : Foreword, Essay
Composer, Music Critic, Music Performance Director

Han Jae Eun : Gimhae Foreign Language High School

Kim On Seong : Gimhae Foreign Language High School

Lee Jeong Eun : Hankuk Academy Of Foreign Studies

Park Jae Woo : Ex-Gimhae Foreign Language High School

Introduction

Introductory Notes

1. The reason 'Corea' not 'Korea' is adopted is that I believe the proper name for my motherland is 'Corea'. Just imagine if 'Canada' was written 'Kanada'.

2. Names of Coreans are written in the way that the family name comes before the first name. For example, 'Hong Gil Dong' means that the family name is 'Hong', the first name is 'Gil Dong'.

3. Native speakers of English have been using 'Shijo' to mean both singular and plural, such as "three Shijo" and "many Shijo". If used as an uncountable noun like 'poetry', it will be like "three pieces of Shijo". In that case we may adopt the Corean poetry counting term, "shoo(pronounced like soup with /p/ sound omitted)". Hence, we could say "three shoos of Shijo". In this book, we are a little confused on the usage of "Shijo". For the time being, the confusion might go on.

4. Capitalized 'Line' refers to one of the three lines of standard Shijo. Hence, we can say that a standard Shijo written in 3 Lines can be displayed in 7 lines.

5. A comma is used as in 'arjirarng'yi' to show that the sounds before and after the comma are not connected. The two are articulated separately, one after the other. So the example does not sound, 'arjirarn-gyi' but 'arjirarng-yi'

6. At the end of this book are attached the translations of the Review, Reflections, Foreword, Editor's Preface, Introduction and Epilogues. The translations are not rounded off to let the readers feel the smell of the original English text.

7. Some translations are credited to the Editor. Some students dropped out before this project was completed. Some of the Shijo once assigned to the dropped students are translated by the Editor himself, from scratch.

On the Romanization of the Corean script

Among many romanization systems, two are dominant. McCune-Reischauer system, which seems to be for the convenience of foreigners, and Corean government system, for that of Coreans. Every several years, this issue surfaces into a hot debate.

I am not satisfied with any of the existing systems. How will the foreigners read 'dam-yang', which is to be read as /dam-jaŋ/ in either romanization system mentioned above? I find many foreigners read it as /dæm-jæŋ/. I guess this problem may be solved if it is written as 'darm-yarng'.

I find it worthwhile and meaningful to present my idea on the romanization. This one may be confusing at first, but if readers give some time to the Explanatory Notes below, they might find this new system reasonable.

Explanatory Notes;

‘e’ is ‘e’ as in ‘desk’.
'ee' is 'ee' as in 'eel'.
‘u’ is ‘e’ as in ‘oven’, 'dozen'.
‘ay’ is ‘a’ as in ‘pack’, 'Jack'.
‘oo’ is ‘oo’ as in ‘soon’, 'good'.
‘er’ is 'er' as in 'her', ‘hermit’ without any r sound.
‘ar’ is ‘ar’ as in ‘dark’, 'sark' without any r sound.
'j' is 'j' as in 'judge'.
's' is 's' as in 'song', 'sing'.
‘sh’ is ‘s’ as in ‘slow’ or ‘sleep’.
'sw' is 'sh' as in 'she', 'shout', 'shirts'.

< Review >

Translation is slow and difficult work, yet so rich and rewarding. I have tasted the difficulty of this work a few times in my life, but none of the poems I have translated were as complex as the Shijo these students, the teacher, and parents labored over. I have just enough empathy to appreciate how wonderful an achievement this publication is. Yet unfortunately not enough to offer a specific insight into the treasures that follow. With this constraint, I offer a few general words.

First, there is no better way to learn the life and idiosyncrasies of a language than to attempt to translate its poetry. Even more so when you translate from your native language into another language, as this publication does. Second, the imagery and emotion of the included Shijo opens up a personal window into each translation. I sense there is as much a story behind each translation as there undoubtedly is to each original composition. Third and lastly, the structure of the Shijo reveals the artistry of the poet and the translator as if they were doing an elegant dance together. While it may appear open and uninhibited in movement and flow, there is a great deal of quiet constraint and technicality. Shijo is every bit as complex as a tango.

With this in mind, I invite the reader to peruse, read, and revisit the artistry contained in the following pages. There is so much to be celebrated here. I congratulate the students, the teacher and family members who shared in this achievement. Thank you for providing a rich English translation of such a beautiful art form.

Amy Levine
Visiting Professor
English Language and Literature
Changwon National University

< Reflections on Shijo >

The revered English poet John Keats once compared the composition of poetry to the budding of leaves on a tree—the idea being that if poetry does not come naturally, it should not come at all. Within this romantically charged metaphor is a conviction that there is something germane to the process of poetic composition. Keats believed that good poetry could not be contrived or manufactured any more than a young sapling can be coaxed to spring its buds in the frigid desolation of winter. It had to come naturally, to spring forth from an inner landscape, to exist in the world with its own arcane reasons for being.

Upon reading this English translation of Corean Shijo, I was struck by the splendor of poetic restraint that comprises some of the outstanding Shijo in this collection. One old Shijo poem in particular by Ser Yik caught my attention for the magnitude of poetic restraint, its rich use of Chinese mythology, and the longing that animates this poem:

> When I've pulled this mountain down,
> and filled up that ocean there,
> I could walk across the ocean,
> to see you at Mt. Bong-nay.
> But I am,
> like the small-girl-turned bird that longed to see her father,
> I wander about before the sea, longing, only longing.

Ser Yik (1542-1587)

The nuances in this poem are rich and captivating. The image of wandering "before the sea" suggests an insurmountable barrier that separates the poet from the object of desire; "before" also signifies as a temporal marker that indicates a permanent condition of longing which has existed before the sea and the formation of geographic boundaries. With the translation, the poem has assumed more nuances because the use of "before" in English has dual meaning as a preposition of both time and place.

The poetic allusions in this poem are based on the Chinese mythology of the lost daughter who has been transformed into a bird. Her father, a god, is desperately seeking her; however, she is unaware of her death, she continually tries to fill the ocean, so she can walk across and be re-united with her father. In the Chosun dynasty many Shijo poems were dedicated to the honor of the King. This poem employs the Chinese myth of the lost daughter to symbolize the poet's longing, and willingness to perform the most impossible tasks, to be acquainted with the King. The poem gathers momentum then unfolds rather ingeniously with the recognition of the subject's existence amidst a fantasy to perform the impossible feat of burying the ocean with the sand of the mountain. The dramatic reversal occurs with the line: "But I am". This recognition of human limitation is as hopeless as it is affirming. The poet is as mythically distant from the King as the lost daughter is from her father.

I came to this collection of Corean Shijo with two predominating impulses; first, I was overtaken by curiosity, I wanted to know why had I never heard of this unique poetic form? Having studied literature in a variety of cultural contexts, I became unsettled by my ignorance of Corean poetry. Indeed, I remember being introduced to the Japanese Haiku and other Eastern poetry in a comparative literature course, we also delved into Zen-Buddhism and the use of Koans. Yet, in my experience of doing both graduate and undergraduate courses in Canada, Corean Shijo was never introduced in our curriculum.

Sadly, there is little knowledge of Corean Shijo. It has demanded little attention from Western scholars; however, this may be changing. The hope that accompanies this fine translation of Corean Shijo, is that it will ignite further interest into this unique and rich poetic form and perhaps spawn more investigations into the powerful mythologies and thematic constructions that comprise Shijo poetry.

The compact use of language, the unveiling of mythological references, and the thematic twists provide Corean Shijo with unique traits that make reading this poetry a great joy. If one envisions the composition of poetry as natural as leaves budding from a tree, then this latest contribution to the long tradition of Corean Shijo demonstrates that this art form is still blooming. Lee Kyung-hoon and the four emerging scholars who labored over this translation have performed a commendable task by bringing this fine poetry to life in English.

William Edwards
M.A. English & Cultural Studies McMaster University
M. Ed. OISE University of Toronto
Former Visiting Professor Changwon National University

< Foreword >

Sadness, the most beautiful moment of Life

How could one go on
without singing a song?
Why is it that sad songs come closer?
Is it that
life is sad by nature?

We, how could we go on
without singing a song?

People sing what they cannot get over. Rather, people sing it because they cannot get over it. In the end, all songs speak about the limitedness of life. We sing songs maybe because our life is limited.

●

A song is a message. So, throughout the songs that touch human hearts, eternity reverberates. Our ancestors contained messages in the form of Shijo. Messages were contained without emotion revealed to the extreme. Emotion deepens, the more it is hidden. Hiding emotion within the uninterested tone is the genuine taste of Shijo. The deeper hidden, the bigger the reversal or ascension in the last Line. So, when I listen to the songs of our ancestors, I come to nod or slap my knee. Sometimes it comes along with immense force.

Jerng Mong-joo and Yi Barng-wern faced each other over some

drinks. After some drinking, Yi Barng-wern sings.

> If it's this way, should it matter?
> If it's that way, then would it matter?
> The hanging vines over'n that Mt. Marnsoo,
> are they to blame for the entanglement?
> Then why not,
> get entangled together,
> to be blessed for a hundred years.

The famous song, “Song of No Matter". He points to the Mt. Marnsoo and sings the life together. But the hidden message was that as Koryo is taken down, and Yi dynasty is built up, they could live together in a new world, a message of temptation. He is referring to a power-sharing deal. The patriot of Koryo senses his impending death in the song. And then, with a vague grin, he sings a song in response.

> Should this body die and die,
> even should die a hundred times
> and should the bones turn to dirt,
> with or without a piece of soul,
> Will it ever,
> cease to be, will it ever go away,
> the single-heart of mine for my lord?

The famous song, 'Song of Purple of Heart'. Through this song, Jerng Mong-joo flatly refuses the proposal, it being impossible to cooperate with those who betrayed the lord and robbed his power. On his way back after the confrontation, he meets his death by the men of Yi Barng-wern.

●

African Americans sing the Blues. Blacks that were emancipated from slavery ultimately fell to the city poor; those who had to survive in the bottom of the society without any protection and those who lived life from crime to prison, their song and their refuge was the Blues. It is astonishing that the Blues has a similar structure as our Shijo. Blacks sang the agony of life in their unique three-line poetry. This verse has developed into the Blues music. Our Shijo, too, when performed as music, turns into Gargok-charng(Shijo-as-song).

The Blues music consists of 12 segments, one line of four segments in four-beat. Shijo, too, consists of three lines, a line of four segments. Therefore, if Shijo should be sung to the Blues' 12 segments, it just fits into it, with no words or segments less or more. The Blues is the testimony of mankind which bloomed from the agonies of life. As the Black's suffering was deeper, the appeal sounds louder in the form of accompaniment or instrumental music. The Blues, born in 20th century, captivated the world with its heartbreaking tone. It also influenced our pop music. From old pop to the present R&B, many songs were born from the Blues.

In the Shijo that we have sung for thousands of years is waiting and missing. I dare predict that our song that is not violent, that does not reveal emotion on the surface, will take not so small a part of the world music in 21st Century. The key lies in the era when the aesthetics of slow is valued as a virtue of life and in the Shijo-singing that lasts for more than 10 minutes with only that short three-line poetry. Our Shijo is also one of the priceless assets of mankind.

Kim Jin-mook

Composer, Music Critic, Music Performance Director

< Artistic class, humane scent and taste of Old Pops >

Kim Jin-mook

When I was a literature loving student, I liked Rainer Maria Rilke. I was fascinated by his meditational poetry compiled in the book: "Duineser Elegien". When he was a young boy, he sang that "I will die in the springtime". I also thought that I wished to die in the Spring. I was enchanted by classical music as well as literature. I liked Schubert and also Lieds by Mahler and Wolff.

On the other hand, I used to be fairly negative toward our own culture. I would turn mad when Hyern Yin in the song: 'Be strong! My dear Kum-soon!' would sing "♬ This very man, is only a peddler, in the Kook-je market ". It just felt too direct and too crude. But as I got older, I suffered the severity of life. I started to change. Because I came to know that the song was the song of desperation in destitution; it was about people looking for their separated family members amid the ultimate struggle for a lump of bread.

Especially the line, " ♩ Up above the parapet of Bridge Yerng-do, the crescent moon is risen lonely now ♬" was impossible to hear without tears. During the Corean War, in their rush to take a refugee, they made an appointment to meet in Busan. As they didn't know much about Busan other than that they heard about the then famous Bridge Yerng-do, so they shouted, "See you again at Bridge Yerng-do". So the refugees gathered in that area to look for their loved ones, lost families and relatives, the bridge being the place of reunion. But, in the evening when the crescent moon is already up in the sky, the loved one, "Kum-soon" never shows up.

In the Old Popular songs, the pain and suffering of our recent history melts. Buried deep in those songs are the grief from the loss of the motherland, the broken hearts from the war between the brothers of the South and North. Historically, Traditional Folk Songs gave birth to the New Folk Songs in the 20th century, which the Western music, in turn, introduced to our popular songs. Amid all these changes and turmoils, the mentality of Coreans never stopped breathing. But songs today are heavily influenced by the Ballads and African-American music like R&B. There are some voices of concern on this social syndrome.

On November 2, at the 'House of Corea' in the Choong-moo street, the Founding Meeting was held for the 'Heart-Felt spanning thousand miles, 유정천리'. It's a small table for the Old Pops, for its artistic status and humane scent and taste. To recover the status deserved by the Old Pops that is now in undue and unfair judgement caused by negative prejudices of some people. Poets, people in the legal profession, in the broadcasting business, in the cultural world, congressmen, and civil offficials and people in various professions gathered to reconfirm its va ue.

Named after the song, 'Heart-Felt spanning thousand miles, 유정천리' by Park Jay-hong, that begins with 'I am going, leaving, hand in hand with my young boy', this meeting planned a variety of businesses: phonograph concerts, the meeting with the Maestro of Old Pops, academic conferences, related materials exhibition and building a museum. Around mid-December at Seoul Arts Center, inviting Ms Kum Sar-hyarng who sang the songs, "A maiden's dream", "A maiden in Hong Kong", they are holding a phonograph concert and a meeting with Old Pop Maestro.

< Editor's Preface >

This book is intended to translate Corean Shijo into English Shijo, not just into English. In the translation, four students took part. This was our process. I selected the Shijo texts to be translated and gave each student a copy. From the list, students selected their favorite Shijo, and sent me their translations. When multiple translations for the same Shijo were submitted, I selected the best one. Translations that were not up to a certain level, even if only one translation was submitted for a Shijo, were not selected. In this way, we assigned Shijo to the students.

In some cases, students' translations were directly added to the finished Shijo list, without any need to revise. In other cases, I reviewed and returned their translations with my opinions attached. In many cases, the translations went back and forth between the students and myself over and over again. I tried my best not to directly intervene in their translation process. I just tried to keep a certain distance, only giving my opinions like, "This word is too formal", "This expression is too direct and unrestrained", "It is not cadence rhymed", etc, because this had to be their translation, not mine. I guess whenever they had their submissions returned with opinions attached, until their translation was added to the list of finished Shijo, they must have felt as if the limit of their patience was being tested. Here, I pay my deepest respect to their hard work and endurance.

At first we had little knowledge about Shijo, much less the English translation of Shijo. Had we known that this work was far from easy, we wouldn't have begun. Any way, we met together, and studied together, in the wake of which, and as time went by, we became better versed in Shijo, and its English translation. We came to understand, little by little, the structure of Shijo and to grasp some understanding of how English Shijo should be. We could get to the understanding of FSTL, SSTL, and also to the display format.

In the beginning, we intended to translate only old Shijo, but scores of modern Shijo are included in this book. Also includec in this book are verses that are not Shijo, but are the works by the authors either who are famous authors of Shijo, or closely related to Shijo. For example, Yoo Hee-gyerng's poems written in Chinese script are included because he was the lover of Yi May-charng. In Part 3, some well known Coreans's favorites are translated.

We'd like to express our deepest gratitude to Poet Min Byeong-do, for his efforts in the procedure of allowing us to translate Shijo by Yi Ho-woo and his sister Poetess Yi Young-do. And also, we deeply appreciate Poet Ban Yung ho for permission to translate his one-Lined Shijo from his poetry book, "Wings of degeneration"(퇴화의 날개). His one-Lined Shijo are in the part of modern Shijo.

We express our sincere and heartfelt thanks to the parents of these 4 students, who for such a long time, stood by us, supported us mentally and financially, gave us strength when we became weak and patiently waited for this book. Without their devotion and cooperation, this book would not have been possible.

We all deeply appreciate Professor Levine for the review. In the review, we could see that she directly got the grasp of Shijo, in such a short period of time. Her review seems to gently assure us that she understands what we have been doing and what we want our readers to read, feel and enjoy. We wish she could have had more time to spare for us.

Students, parents and myself would like to express our heart-felt gratitude to William Edwards, who proofread our work so thoroughly, offered insightful feedback and so valuable comments and even wrote reflections for us. He did a very thorough work, without overlooking anything, covering all the minor details including even typos. It was an amazing experience to see our work, with his comments and reflections, evolve into something bigger and deeper. Personally I was deeply impressed with his professional work. And I confess that the introduction is rewritten after I received his comments. As I added a little more and made some small corrections after he finished his comments, there may be some grammatical errors. If there should be any, the errors are mine.

We are really honored to have a foreword by the famous music critic, composer, music producer, music columnist, art director, and world music expert, Kim Jin-mook. He is the first Jazz critic in Corea and well known for his great expertise in world music, all kinds of different music of the world, an expert on ethnic music and tribal music. To express our appreciation, I translated one of his essays from his blog:

http://cafe.naver.com/carvonism.cafe

The title of his essay is “Artistic class, humane scent and taste of Old Popular Songs”. It is right after his foreword.

I'd like to express many thanks to the Professors and scholars devoted to the study of English Shijo. Reading their papers and books, I was able to build up my own knowledge and perspect ve. Without their foregoing study, this book would have been just another translation book.

Here, we hope that this book will be of some help to foreigners interested in Corean culture. We believe that reading Shijo, old and modern, will be an extremely effective way of understanding Corea and Corean people. We also hope that what we've been through making this book will be something helpful to those interested in English Shijo. Also expected is that Middle School and High School students will get some help from this book in their better understanding of Shijo and the English language.

I will deeply appreciate if whoever is interested in English Shijo or in English gives feedback or comments, good or bad, through my e-mail address: taran707@gmail.com or taran707@naver.com

< Introduction >

Before we go into details, let's have a little taste with a bite of Shijo, first. Below is displayed a 'shoo' of Shijo in seven lines, each line in two segments.

Having left my fair lord,
far away and far apart,
I sat alone at a stream,
'cause I had nowhere to put my heart.
The water there,
must be like my heart walking
along the dark path, sobbing and weeping.

Let's see how to read it. It is to be read like this. Take a pause at "//".

Having left // my fair lord,
far away // and far apart,
I sat alone // at a stream,
'cause I had nowhere // to put my heart.
The water there, //, //, //
must be like my heart, walking
along the dark path, // sobbing and weeping.

We can see that it is in 12 segments. The time duration for each segment is the same. Three "//"s are marked after "The water there", which means that longer pause is required here. We notice that the sixth line, "must be like my heart, walking" is longer than other segments and that there is no "//" in that line. This means that this line has to be read in one stroke without any pause or hesitation in the middle and a little faster to be finished in the same time duration with other shorter segments. If read aloud, a certain kind of rhythm or cadence will be felt through. That rhythm or cadence is the characteristic of Shijo. And it is the indispensable element of Shijo that the sixth line is longer but must be read in one stroke, without any pause and in the same time duration.

Why a new one?

All Coreans know what Shijo is. Difficult theories on Shijo may be only for professional scholars, but there will be no Corean adult who cannot memorize and murmur one or two Shijo. There will be no one who cannot tell if the given text is Shijo or not, if it's not borderline cutting-edge modern Shijo. The problem lies in English Shijo. It is widely believed, at least in Corea, that the biggest reason Shijo is not well known compared to Japanese Haiku, is the lack of publicity. But I guess the biggest reason lies in the fact that we haven't presented "what Shijo is" in simple English.

I notice, in some Shijo websites by Westerners, some lingering thirst for an understanding of what Shijo is and what Shijo is not. For example, we all know that a Line of Shijo cannot be dividable in odd number of segments, for example, in three or five segments. We do not consider them as Shijo. But some Westerners would write them and consider them as Shijo.

We all know well what the "reversal" in the last Line means. We know that the SSTL(the second segment in the last Line) needs to be longer than other segments, but pronounced in the same time period with other shorter segments, which brings in the unique taste of Shijo, without which we cannot consider the text as Shijo. OK, then, those works translated in English and those originally written in English, do they carry that same taste of Shijo, the reversal in the last Line or something similar with that? To our disappointment, current English Shijo and English-translated Corean Shijo are not much different from English poetry only written in three lines. If we cannot present an answer to this question, "Is it really different from 3-line English poetry?", there is no English Shijo.

This book presents our own solutions to these problems. Of course, this book does not give all the necessary answers. We expect professional scholars to provide more advanced contributions. And after some time from now, after some basic theories in English Shijo is set up and becomes stable, English Shijo will be up to the English speakers, no more to the Coreans. At that time, English Shijo will go its own way, the way we never know for now.

About Shijo

Corea is a country of long history, at least 5,000 years old, thus she is enriched with diverse cultural legacies and one of which is Shijo. The root of Shijo is generally accepted to date back at least to 14th century A.D., which is during the Koryo dynasty (AD 918

~ 1392), from which the name "Corea" is derived. Among several traditional fixed verse forms that appeared in the literary history of Corea, only Shijo survives, being written and published today. There are more than 1,000 Shijo poets in Corea. The latest dictionary of Shijo by Park Ul-soo(박을수) published in 1991, contains a total of 5,492 pieces.

Other forms (one example: Karsar, sister to Shijo) are not completely dead. The Karsar is being written, but it is not being considered as a literary accomplishment. Therefore, there are Shijo poets but no Karsar poets. Like Shijo, Karsar was performed with instrumental accompaniment. Shijo was called tarn'gar(short song) and Karsar was called jarng'gar(long song).

The Karsar is also rhymed by cadence and repetition of 3+4 syllables, but different from Shijo in that; (1) Shijo is definitely a kind of verse, a poetry form. Karsar is not prose because it is rhymed. But also it cannot be easily categorized as a verse. It is prose written in the form of verse. A good example of Karsar would be the Bible re-written in Karsar format. (2) Whereas Shijo is limited to 3 Lines, Karsar has no limit. It can be written in as many as 40 lines or more. Shijo is constrained in 3 Lines, Karsar speaks out. (3) Shijo in the narrow sense requires in the last Line, a reversal in terms of cadence and meaning. Cadence is changed from the previous two Lines. The last line in most cases reveals the writer's inner feelings and concludes the whole Shijo. Karsar do not require this reversal. Yoon Sern-do's 'Fishermen's four seasons', the famous linked Shijo of 40 verses, is sometimes categorized as a Karsar, all 40 verses as one Karsar.

Some people contend that Karsar should be revived. Im Jong-Chan, in the paper “A Speculation on the Prospect and

Globalization of Modern Sijo(현대시조의 진로모색과 세계화 문제 연구), published in 2005", states that Karsar should be revived as a genre of modern literature saying that it is too good to be lost.

Well, Shijo was revived because some people first made the argument that Shijo should be revived, and other people agreed on it. Maybe some day Karsar might be restored. If Shijo is a slim and good looking, somewhat sensitive young woman, Karsar would be a well-socialized, weight-gained middle aged man. Shijo needs the writer's personal inner feelings revealed, diretcly or indirectly. But it is just an option in Karsar. So, Karsar will be a good form in which to write things political, religious and educational.

Please note that this kind of gender difference analogy, which I have never seen, is my own personal feelings of an amateur on the two different traditional genres. It's an analogy focused on, (1) Shijo reveals personal feelings when Karsar doesn't have to, (2) Shijo has to use some technical reversal in the final Line when Karsar does not.

The word 'Shijo'

Sometimes it is written as 'sijo'. We adopted 'Shijo' to make sure that 'sh' should not be pronounced as 's' in 'sea', 'see', but 's' as in 'sleep', 'slow', 'sliver'. 'Shi' means time, season. 'Shi-jo' is 'jo' of 'shi'. 'Jo' is the word being used today. Lamenting tone, show-offy tone will translate into "harntarn-jo"and "jar-rarng-jo", respectively. Coreans use the word 'jo' in other ways, too. "This poem is in 4.4. jo" means: "This poem is written in the form of 4 syllables + 4 syllables". We can say Shijo is a verse of 3.4. jo. “Jo” is also used in music. Corean traditional music, too, has major and minor. It is called "pyerng-jo"(comparable to major in Western music) and "kye-myern-jo"(comparable to minor in Western music). Hence, 'Shijo' is 'jo' of time, 'jo' of the season.

Definition

It is not easy to give a clear definition of Shijo. What is referred to by the word 'Shijo' is not singular. It refers to textual verses and also to songs performed by professional Shijo singers with instrumental accompaniment, which we may call Shijo-as-song. It also refers to the musical melodies used in Shijo-as-song. There's another reason. There are many varieties of Shijo. What is discussed is mainly normal, common or standard Shijo, which is often called pyerng-Shijo in Corean. If there are other kinds of Shijo, then what exactly is Shijo? Actually, this question seems to be quite difficult to answer. These questions arise because Shijo began as a song. The questions are related to Shijo-as-music.

As we cannot go into details here, a brief remark would suffice. Kargok-charng, which is Shijo performed and sung with instrumental accompaniment, has had various kinds of texts as its lyrics including even Chinese poetry. Hence, we can say that kargok-charng is an empty bowl; it can contain almost any lyrical form. In that case, what is Shijo would not surface above the water. Shijo as textual lyric poetry is independent from music, at this point the issue surfaces. Shijo as song is beyond this writer's ability, hence we will mainly be focused on Shijo as textual verse, mainly pyerng-Shijo, normal standard Shijo.

The definition of Shijo as a textual verse is well summarized by Professor Cho Dong-il, probably the best known and most important literature theorist in Corea. The following is my translation of his explanation(His book, "History of Corean literature", volume 2, p187, 한국문학통사).

> The question on the origin of Shijo should be settled according to the definition of Shijo. If Shijo is what is composed of three Lines(capitalized Line refers to one of three lines of a Shijo), a Line of four segments, a segment of standard four syllables, we've had it for a long time. Some songs of Bayk-je dynasty(BC 18 ~ AD 660) or Koryo dynasty(AD 918 ~ AD 1392) were in this format.
>
> This format sometimes appears in what is written as modern poetry, too. The three-Line format existed in any given period of literary history [in Corea], because it was a variant of four-Line, thus it was not perceived as an independent literary genre. But a name was still required for it, thus 'pseudo-Shijo' was offered, but I think 'Shijo in the broad sense' is a proper name.
>
> If one more condition is added to the 'Shijo in the broad sense', the condition being the first segment of the third Line is composed of one or two syllables less than the average four syllables and the second segment is composed of one or two more than the average four, this is the 'Shijo in the narrow sense'. That special device allowed Shijo some solid structure which made it possible to finish within three Lines, with no need to go on into four Lines. The 'Shijo in the broad

> sense' is born naturally, whereas 'Shijo in the narrow sense' is made intentionally from 'Shijo in the broad sense'.
>
> The exclamatory remark at the beginning of the last Line used in Hyarng-gar(鄕歌, literally local songs) during Shilla dynasty(BC 57 ~ AD 935), which gave tension on the finish, was not lost in the course of renovative development toward 'Shijo in the narrow sense'.
>
> ...
>
> But simply casting doubts on the credibility of Shijo in the late Koryo period cannot be an option, because there are many extant Shijo and Shijo writers [presumed to have written Shijo in that period]. It is valid to understand that there arose a restructuring of the literature in that period, bringing in a new type of lyric poetry.

The definition we saw above by Professor Cho Dong-il is about pyerng-Shijo, normal or standard Shijo.

Structure

1. Fundamentals

The standard syllable count of a standard Corean Shijo has often been presented as:

	12-segment	6-segment
First Line	3 + 4 + 3 + 4	7+7
Second Line	3 + 4 + 3 + 4	7+7
Last Line	3 + 5 + 4 + 3	8+7

We see that, in case of 12-segment, the basic syllable count in a Shijo is 3+4, 3 syllables followed by 4 syllables, which is the way Corean language is spoken. Corean language, in extreme roughness, could be said to be a language of 3+4. Shijo could be summed up as a song of 3+4, a repetition of 3+4. We need to take a note that the cadence or syllable count in the last Line is changed from the two previous Lines, which is '3+5'[4 of the second segment is lengthened to 5 or more], followed by 4+3[3+4 is reversed]. It should not be overlooked that the syllable count change in the last Line is compulsory, as long as it is 'Shijo in the narrow sense', which we call 'Shijo' today. Thus, the last Line is given some special status. In terms of meaning, as it finishes a Shijo, revealing the writer's inner feelings, some kind of reversal in the meaning is also necessary or inevitable. This special status of the last Line has been referred to as a 'twist and turn', or 'reversal', etc.

As we have seen above, Shijo is widely accepted to be the fixed verse form composed of three Lines, each Line of four segments, a segment of four syllables on average, the first segment of the third Line(herein after, "FSTL") is in three syllables, and the second segment of the third Line(herein after, "SSTL") is lengthened to more than 4 syllables, for the purpose of reversal in terms of cadence. However, there is another theory. Kim Jeong Hwa(김정화), in the paper, "Characteristics of Shijo in the form(published in the year 2003), 시조의 형태적 특질", proposes a very different, but noteworthy opinion.

> (1) Shijo is composed of 4 Lines, not of three Lines, because the FSTL is a separate Line composed of the lone segment. The lone segment is the characteristic of verse forms in Corea as is shown in Hyarng gar[which were popular in Shilla dynasty]. (2) There is no reason that the FSTL should be in 3 syllables. The three syllabled ness had been developed and introduced out of cadential and rhythmic necessity, not from some inevitable poetic theory. (3) The statement that the SSTL is given more syllable count than other segments turns out to be meaningless, because it is not one segment, but the first two segments of the fourth Line. (4) The FSTL deserves the status of a separate Line because it often ends in a vowel, thus it is easy to be pronounced in a lengthened manner.

This theory is very fresh, interesting and thought- provoking. But the theory has to be supported by some substantial proof. Let's take a closer look. First, do the FSTLs end in vowels? Park Ul soo's Corea Shijo dictionary(한국시조대사전), out of one hundred pieces from number 1 to 100, nineteen pieces have FSTLs not ending in vowels. It's about 80%. Let's ask Hwarng Jin yi, the number one Shijo master in the whole history of Shijo. Among her six pieces of surviving Shijo, five pieces have FSTLs ending in a vowel, which is 83%. Hence, we can say that about 80% of FSTLs end in vowels. So, in this regard, the author's argument is justified.

How about syntax? If the FSTL is not syntactically independent, the theory that it is a separate Line composed of one segment seems to be groundless because in that case it is just a part of another Line. Exclamatory or rather pattern-phrased FSTLs are per se independent. In Park Ul soo's Corea Shijo dictionary(한국시조대사전), only 62 among the first 200 verses had that syntactically independent, lone segment. It is only 31%, and none of Hwang Jin yi's six Shijo have the syntactically independent FSTLs. With all things considered, a lone segment, a separate Line theory doesn't seem to be on a firm ground.

There is one more point to mention here. A "Line" is divided into segments for the consideration of pause. After each segment, a pause is expected. The argument by Kim Jeong Hwa, that the SSTL is not one segment as has been understood, but two separate segments is difficult to agree upon. It seems not to emphasize the reversal or 'twist and turn' in the Last Line, which should be the core of Shijo.

If the SSTL is articulated in two segments, with a pause in-between, then what happens? There is no reversal, no 'twist and turn', just plain and dull continuation of segments. The reversal or 'twist and turn' lies where SSTL is longer than other segments, but articulated in one segment, with no pause in-between. According to the argument by Kim Jeong Hwa, the reversal, or 'twist and turn', or change of cadence in the Last Line gets plainly lost. This is why I find it difficult to agree with this theory by Kim Jeong Hwa. But the theory gives us some insight, at least, on the special status of FSTL and SSTL.

2. The nature of the syllable count cadence

Corean language is not a language of tones like Chinese, nor a language of accents like English. Tones and accents do not make a difference in the meaning of words. Hence, Coreans developed cadence in terms of syllable count.

3. The meaning of the Fixed Form

Though it is in fixed form, the degree of fixedness is not as strict as Japanese Haiku or Chinese Quatrain. There is some flexibility other than that it is composed of 3 Lines, each Line of 4 segments, each segment of standard 4 syllables, the first segment of the third Line should be composed of 3 syllables, the second segment not less than 5 syllables and no more than 8. Each segment can be longer or shorter than the standard structure presented above, by the margin of 1~2 syllables or in some cases to 3 syllables, especially in the case of SSTL. Due to this flexibility, Shijo is called a verse in "imperfect fixed form".

4. 6 segments vs 12 segments

(1) Basics

a. number of Lines

There is no doubt that Shijo takes the form of three Lines. The number of Lines cannot be four or more than four. It has to be in three Lines. But there can be one-Lined Shijo and two-Lined Shijo. These two variants are experimental, at least until today. It is not a widely accepted form of Shijo, yet. But one thing sure is that the two variants give some insight into the definition of Shijo. We have Poet Ban Yung ho's one-Lined Shijo here.

b. even number of segments in one Line

We have to bear in mind that no Lines of Shijo can be in three segments or five segments. The number of segments in one Line has to be two or four. It's a firmly set rule, regardless of the number of Lines, at least in pyerng-shijo, common standard shijo.

c. same time duration for each segment

The time duration for each segment in one Shijo is the same. All the segments must be pronounced or read in the same time frame. This means that the segments consisted of more syllables must be pronounced in somewhat hurried manner to meet the timeline. Also we need to be reminded that each segment needs to be balanced in terms of syllable count. One segment cannot be longer than the other by too big a margin. If there's no limit of duration for a segment, then there is no point in fixed formed ness, no point in syllable count, no point in rhythm and cadence.

d. arbitrary Line break

The Line break is arbitrary. Each reader may break the same Line of the same Shijo at a different place. It is arbitrary but cannot be too arbitrary because the time duration is the same among all the segments in one Shijo.

(2) What is the difference?

"Of how many segments a piece of Shijo must be composed" or "Into how many segments a piece of Shijo must be breakable" is the subject of hot debate. There are two opinions; the 6-segmentism and the 12-segmentism. The 12-segmentism seems to have been prevailing in the Shijo both old and modern.

Then, what is the difference between the 6-segmentism and the 12-segmentism? If it's 6 segments, a piece of Shijo may be considered well done if each Line is breakable only in two separate segments and further breaking of a Line is not necessary. In that case, the fixed form structure becomes a lot looser, for the writer is allowed more freedom. But if it's 12 segments, the writer has to see to it that each Line is breakable into four separate segments, each segment given about the same duration of time, thus he is given less freedom.

Let's take a closer look. Jang Kyung-Ryul, in his essay, 'An essay on English translation of Shijo, published in 2005, 시조의 영역을 위한 하나의 시론(試論) - 현대비평과 이론 24호', states that :

> (1) Though it is not strictly adhered to, there will be no one that will object to the theory that Shijo is a fixed-form verse that consists of 3 Lines, six segments and 43 syllables(p 177).
> (2) We have to look into ourselves if our Shijo poets' awareness of Shijo remains only at the level that Shijo is just a fixed form verse that consists of 3 Lines, 6 segments and 43 syllables(p182).

It is true that no one will object to the theory of 3 Lines or six segments. However, it is far from sure whether most Coreans will agree that the 'six segments' is enough. In fact, many people seem to believe that a shoo of Shijo must be breakable into 12 segments and that being breakable only into 6 segments is not enough. Rather, the 12-segmentism seems to be prevailing now. Focused on pyerng-Shijo(standard Shijo), we can easily see that it is really the 12-segmentism that is being widely supported. Why? Because it is hard to find Shijo, old or modern, written in 6 segments, not dividable into 12 segments. It is not sure if the author supports the six-segmentism in the sense that he considers it unnecessary for a shoo of Shijo to be breakable into 12 segments.

The author presents his own translation of the Shijo by Yi Sayk as below, adding the remark that the six-line display is meant to reflect the intention to be faithful to the 6-segment structure of Shijo.

In the valley of deep snows
    The clouds are cold and dreary;
Oh, lovely plum flowers,
    Where are you blooming now?
Standing alone at sunset,
    I am wondering where to go.

Now, let's see what the difference is, the difference between the 6-segmentism and the 12-segmentism. This translation will break into 12 segments as below:

In the valley // of deep snows
    The clouds are // cold and dreary;
Oh, lovely plum flowers,
    Where are you // blooming now?
Standing alone // at sunset,
    I am wondering // where to go.

The third line, "Oh, lovely plum flowers" will be either, (A) "Oh, lovely // plum flowers" or (B) "Oh, // lovely plum flowers". In (A), the line break looks too arbitrary. An English speaker's natural sense of Line break will be (B). In the case of (B), then "lovely plum flowers" is too long compared with "Oh". Looked in the 12-segmentism, this "Oh" is a segment that consists of one syllable.

Here, in the 12-segmentism, we come to the question: Can a segment consist of one syllable, like 'Ah!' or 'Oh!'? This is a question that never arises in the 6-segmentism. A segment consisted of one syllable is very rare in Shijo. In Park Ul-soo's Corea Shijo dictionary(한국시조대사전), from the Shijo number 1 to 200, there is no segment consisted of one syllable. Im Jong-Chan, in the book, "Speculation on the Modern Shijo(현대시조 탐색), published in 2009", states that a segment consisted of one syllable should not be allowed. I agree on that theory of Im Jong-Chan.

Here, we can see that 6-segmentism gives a writer more freedom. But Shijo written in 12-segments give more sense of rhythm and cadence and sound more lively. As we believe Shijo should be in 12 separate segments, we tried to strictly stick to the 12-segmentism.

5. FSTL, the first segment of the third Line

(1) The nature of FSTL

In some old Shijo, the first segment of the last Line would consist of patterned phrases, like 'let it be', 'my dear lad', 'I'd rather', 'perhaps', 'how can you', 'in truth', 'like this', 'from where', 'among them', 'no matter how', 'erzber'(meaning ah!), etc. These patterned phrases, we may call 'universal phrases', 'set phrases' or 'regulated phrases'.

Some scholars give the impression that FSTL was dominated by these universal phrases. Jo Tae Seong(조태성), in his paper 'An essay on translation into a foreign language of Si-jo, 시조의 외국어 번역에 관한 시론(published in 2009)', adopting the term, "regulated words", states that:

> regulated words in the FSTL is accepted by everybody as an indispensible element that makes Shijo Shijo-like. The regulated words should be used in FSTL both in modern creative Shijo and also in the translation into foreign languages, reason being, if it is not so, it can be difficult to know whether the given text is Shijo or not. If regulated words are not used in the FSTL, the Shijo-like-ness will weigh down.

We need to look if patterned phrases dominated the FSTL, as the author makes his argument. We see that that was not the case. In Park Ul-soo's Corea Shijo dictionary(한국시조대사전), only 62 among the first 200 verses had that patterned phrases in the FSTL. It is only 31%. This fact clearly brings doubt to the so-called exclamatory or set phrased nature of the FSTL. What

the essay proposes is quite to the extreme. In addition, the essay gives the opinion that FSTL should be in 3 syllables only.
How about modern Shijo? Modern Shijo hardly uses patterned phrases. But what the author proposes does not seem to be meaningless. If Shijo is an imperfect fixed form, that kind of limit on that segment could be of some merit. As mentioned in his essay, with patterned phrases in FSTL, readers could easily see that it is written as Shijo or intended as Shijo.

But, that considered, binding Shijo in that patterned phrases may, very likely, shrink Shijo, putting on too much of a burden. It might block the easy flow and also might shrink down the explosive poetic senses and ideas. Shijo might turn out to be some kind of enervated, adynamic and suffocating poetic binder. When we can have two options, why give up one? The problem the essay proposes can be dealt with by other solutions. And also, we should not forget that modern Shijo does not need patterned phrases in the FSTL. Our way of solution will be offered later at the Display Format Section.

(2) The three-syllable structure of FSTL

Yi Ho-woo, probably the top modern Shijo writer, who is widely viewed to have advanced Shijo to a new level with his sister Yi Young-do, where he needed to write 'grandfather'(할아버지), the 4-syllable word in Corean language, shortened it to 3 syllables(할버지), which no one would use if not a small kid barely out of babbling period. This example shows how seriously the first segment of the last Line is being taken, even among Shijo writers today.

But in textual Shijo poetry and also Shijo-as-song, there doesn't seem to be any inevitable reason that the FSTL has to be in three syllables. I admit that I could not find out why the FSTL has been put under the tradition of three syllables. I only guess it has been a tradition. Professor Cho Dong-il gives us a hint. He writes in his book, the exclamatory remark in the last Line was used in Hyarng-gar during Shilla dynasty. Linguistically, exclamatory remarks in Corean language are, in most cases, in three syllables.

Among the first 400 verses in Park Ul-soo's Shijo dictionary, only 17 shoos of Shijo do have FSTL not consisted of three syllables. How about in English Shijo? FSTL has to be in three syllables? If we fix it at three syllables in English Shijo, I guess more loss is expected than gain, because unlike Corean language, exclamatory remarks in English do not tend to be in 3 syllables. Therefore, we have to give more freedom to English Shijo. But it doesn't mean that the special status of FSTL is not necessary in English, nor that FSTL can be lengthened without limit. Further details will be addressed in the Display Format section.

6. The reversal in the last Line

One thing that deserves our attention and is probably the most important in the structure, is the reversal, often referred to as 'twist and turn', in the third Line. This is orthodox and traditional. This reversal or 'twist and turn', lies not only in the form but also in the meaning. The SSTL is lengthened, giving the reader a change of tone, suggesting the impending climax and finale. The easy and non - hesitant flow, arriving right before the end, speeds up to have more to say and tapers off at the end.

As mentioned above, Cho Dong-il classifies between 'Shijo in the narrow sense' and 'Shijo in the broad sense' in terms of the syllable count change in the FSTL and SSTL. In the above mentioned book, he writes that "Shijo that has FSTL consisted of either standard three syllables or less and SSTL of five or six syllables which is more-than-standard syllable count, are Shijo in the narrow sense". Here, looked in different perspective, we can see that he makes a distinction between the two varieties of Shijo in terms of whether or not there is some speed-up in the final Line, because more syllables require faster reading, each segment being given the same time duration. This reversal, at least in the form, if not in meaning, is an indispensible part of Shijo. Thus, Cho Dong-il classifies Yoon Sern-do's 'fishermen's four seasons' as 'Shijo in the broad sense', not as 'Shijo in the narrow sense', because that Shijo lacks the reversal in the last Line.

But, considering the importance of the last Line, we can see that the SSTL seems to be a little short of fulfilling its mission. If it's really about reversal, the change from 3+4 to 3+5 is simply way too weak, too minimal. The change and the difference are not very conspicuous. It's an incomplete device. This incompleteness, I guess, comes from the fact that Shijo started as song. In musical performance, the difference might have been conspicuous. Given this undistinguished nature of the SSTL, it's not that easy to understand why it is being emphasized so much. Is it really such a big deal, the change from 3+4 to 3+5? In modern Shijo, as the syllable count limit is getting a lot more loosened and longer syllables are frequently used, the difference and contrast is all the less sensed, thus the SSTL being not much different from other segments.

If the contrast and difference is not fully felt through, Shijo turns to be a little boring. It might as well just turn into three lined poetry. So, it might not be too harsh if we say that Shijo today seems to be a mere repetition of ancient tradition, a tradition repeated when its mother, the Shijo music, is lost. Like an orphan confined in a tradition, Shijo, once assisted by music, is now forced to stand alone, without much to defend itself. It's no wonder that Shijo is not very popular today in Corea. People do not read Shijo very much. The repetition of 3+4 syllables, unless extremely well written, easily invites the feeling of cliché and monotony. People like free verse more, which was introduced under the influence of western free verse.

Something special in the third Line is necessary and essential. To make the change of tone more apparent and distinguished, without the help of music, the SSTL needs to be lengthened a lot more, enough for the difference or unbalance to be read, heard and felt loud and clear. If the FSTL gets longer than 3 syllables, for example to 5 syllables, then the SSTL, in proportion, has to get a lot longer, maybe to about 10~12 syllables? This clear change of tone will definitely bring more fun, besides setting the identity and independence of Shijo on firmer footing. Maybe we should never forget that the music, mother of Shijo-as-verse is gone. It does not mean that Shijo as song is not being performed any more. It does mean that today's Shijo are being written not as lyrics devoted to musical performance, but are being written as independent poetry. The place that was once taken by the music is void now and has to be filled with something else. Until now, the place is not fully filled up. The change to 3+5 from 3+4 is not enough. The SSTL has to be lengthened significantly to make its presence more distinguished. We tried to reflect this special nature of SSTL in the translation, that SSTL needs to get much longer compared to other segments.

7. Patterned Phrase as the third Line

In many old Shijo, apart from the patterned phrase in the FSTL, the whole third Line was patterned phrase. Lee Yim Su, in the paper, "Verification on the patternization of the last Line - 시조 종장의 관용화 현상에 대한 검증, published in 1992", showed the result of his research. The result was that out of 682 Shijo, which is about 1/7 of all old Shijo, 89 Shijo or 13 %, had a third Line composed of patterned phrases. So we see that more than 10 % of old Shijo had the patternized third Line.

8. The last Line is the conclusion of Shijo

The last Line, looked from another perspective, always gives the conclusion. The reversal of the form and the meaning in the last Line translates into the conclusion of the Shijo. In most cases, good Shijo requires the writer's clear conclusion. The reason might come from the fact that it was mainly started by the new literati, who began to rise from the late Koryo dynasty. They seem to have written Shijo for political or ideological reasons. So, a conclusion was needed. The political reasons were either to ask for the king's favor for the writer himself or to express personal complaints on the world, or to express Confucian ideology.

9. Easy Flow

As Shijo were written to be sung to music, easy flow was an indispensable part of Shijo. Modern Shijo too, though never conscious of being sung, reflects this tradition well. Good Shijo flows smoothly. Hence, it is not difficult, it is light-hearted, it does not try to hide something, it does not try highly sophisticated techniques. To allow easy flow, punctuation marks like colons or semicolons are usually avoided, unless they are urgently necessary.

10. Enjambment

T.S. Eliot used enjambment in the opening lines of his poem 'The Waste Land':

> April is the cruelest month, breeding
> Lilacs out of the dead land, mixing
> Memory and desire, stirring
> Dull roots with spring rain.
> Winter kept us warm, covering
> Earth in forgetful snow, feeding
> A little life with dried tubers.

To be focused on our topic, let us define the "enjambment" to be the technique that the final segment of a "Line" works as a part of the next "Line". Enjambment in terms of "lines" not of "Lines" is much used in this book, as we adopted seven-line display. The technique, "enjambment in terms of Lines" rarely appears in old Shijo. A clear and outstanding exception is the Shijo by Hwarng Jin-yi, "Oh, my, did I not know" on page 188, although that technique is not carried in our English translation.

11. Sophisticated Enjambment

There can be a technique that we may call 'Sophisticated Enjambment'. Whereas "enjambment" is a mere physical technique of displaying words, this technique is a lot more advanced. In this technique, a segment can be understood to be connected to either the previous segment or the following one, making sense in both cases, thus bringing in rich and multiple implications.

Look at the upper Shijo on the page 193. In Corean original Shijo, the last segment of the second Line can be understood as a part of either the second Line, meaning "Would he have bothered to go?", or of the third Line, which is an example of an enjambment, meaning "I did bother to have him go and then I am missing him now". Actually it may have been intended to mean both. This is an amazing technique. The writer didn't want to have him go but happened to do so, and he didn't mean to go but he had to, for some reason. Within strictly limited fixed form, the writer vividly pictures to us this complicated situation and complicated two minds, using this highly sophisticated enjambment technique. Isn't it amazing in the 16th Century, there was a Shijo writer commanding that highly sophisticated technique?

We have the same sophisticated enjambment in English translation in this book. Look at the page 178.

> The two Buddha, naked and starved
> face each other, on the road
> rain or wind, snow or frost
> they will only have to suffer.
> They never know,
> human separation,
> I do envy those two Buddha.

"rain or wind, snow or frost" could be understood either as a part of the previous two lines, meaning (A) the two Buddha face each other whether it “rains or winds, snows or frosts” or as a part of the next line, meaning (B) they will have to, without any way of getting out, suffer rain or wind, snow or frost. Thus, it can contain one of the two meanings or both.

12. Enjambment in terms of verses

Does the third Line always have to be the conclusion of a Shijo, finishing the Shijo? Present day Shijo in linked verses tend to allow the third Line not to finish the Shijo, thus it is semantically and syntactically connected to the next verse, working as if it is the first Line of the next verse linked. It can be called "enjambment in terms of verses".

Is this "enjambment in terms of verses" to be allowed? Well, many contest winners today are written in that style. We may say that Shijo written in that style is not written in three Lines. It is only displayed in 3 Lines, because the last Line is actually the first Line of the next piece of Shijo linked. If it’s allowed, the writer is given more freedom, having two options. Then, how important is the three lined structure of Shijo? I’d like to stand with the conservatives. The last Line must be the conclusion and be self-contained, not acting as a part of the first Line of the verses linked.

Display Format

Shijo can be broken into three parts or three stichs. If a verse cannot be broken into three parts, it is not a Shijo. Of course we have two Lined Shijo and one Lined Shijo. But here we are referring to only common standard Shijo. Each of the three parts is called a Line. We use capitalized 'Line' to refer to the three parts of a Shijo. Into how many lines, a Shijo should be displayed is also a subject of controversy.

As music accompanied old Shijo, it is believed to have been displayed in five parts. Of course many Shijo were written without any consideration on the space between characters, which is not allowed in modern Corean writing. Some say that Shijo as text were displayed in five parts in consideration for kargok-charng, the musical performance of Shijo with instrumental accompaniment. On this argument, that textual Shijo was displayed in five separate parts, I personally have some doubt. If you actually listen to the kargok-charng, you will strongly feel that it is in 2 parts, before an interlude, and after. So, the 5-part display may have been something accidental, not compulsory. I mean, that kind of display may not have been wide spread at that time, but it is found later today, in one or two books only. The ground of my argument is that the evidence presented by the 5-part-display followers is no more than one book, the kum-ok-chong-boo by Arn Min-yerng, during Chosun dynasty.

Today, the display format also comes to attention. I guess it should be something up to the writer, but some scholars argue different opinions. Kevin O'Rourke, who translated some Corean literary works, thus often hailed as 'a missionary of Corean literature', says that "five-line English format corresponds broadly with the five-part structure of the kagok ch'ang to which the songs were originally sung"

Jo Tae Seong(조태성), in his paper 'An essay on translation into a foreign language of Si-jo, published in 2009', states that Arn Min-yerng's book 'kum-ok-chong-boo' written during Chosun dynasty, is quoted to have said that all the verses in the book are displayed in the five-line format for the consideration of Gargok singing. And then he asserts that five-line format is the way of translating Shijo into English to reveal the unique formal characteristics of Shijo.

The five-line format is being displayed in the manner that the first Line of a Shijo is displayed in the first two lines, the second Line in the third line, the FSTL in the fourth line and the rest in the last line. Does that five line format look better? It is difficult to agree. If the five line format was developed for Shijo-as-music, Gargok, then this question surfaces. Now that Shijo is independent from music, why go back to it? Isn't it regressive? Shijo cannot be some kind of subordinate to the music, which might have been the case in the old time. Shijo verse is itself independent with an independent identity. Then, why decide Shijo verse according to the old form?

The six-line format was adopted by Richard Rutt, Kim Jaihyun and the former foreign minister and Prime Minister Y. T. Pyun in 'SONGS FROM KOREA' published in 1948. This six-line format now seems to have settled down as a standard form of Shijo translation into English.

Kevin O'Rourke says in his book, 'The book of Korean Shijo', "The five-line format, however, does have its problems. The most obvious is the fourth line, which is normally not semantically independent. I have had to reach an accommodation between musical development and the truncated three-syllable literary text".

Jo Tae Seong also states in the above mentioned paper that:

> "The FSTL carries out either purely exclamatory or some meaningful function. The first case causes no problem in English translation [because it is syntactically independent]. But in the second case, there comes the dilemma. If it's purely exclamatory, it may be replaced by any expression. But in the other case, it will be difficult to use a patterned phrase in translation [as I think that the FSTL has to be in patterned phrase], where original Shijo used syntactically meaningful segment, [because doing so will change the meaning of the original Shijo .]

Definitely, the separate display of FSTL brings more beauty and fun. At least it matches well with the special status of the FSTL in the whole poem. Without the special status of FSTL and without the twist and turn in the SSTL, how can Shijo be distinguishable from other kinds of verses? Can it be very different from a 3 Lined free verse only written within some syllable count boundary? If the FSTL is displayed in a separate Line, the reader or reciter will, after the FSTL, take pause, longer than the one between other segments. Then the audience will anticipate what will follow next. The pause will bring in a sense of Shijo ness, a unique poetry form, both in form and in recitation.

To occupy a separate line, the FSTL needs to secure some independence syntactically and semantically. But it doesn't have to be 100% independent. Examples like, "I'd rather", "What can I", "Whoever else', "Let it be", "What more is", "Who would not", etc, are good candidates for FSTL.

Conclusion of Display Format

We adopted a seven-line format. The FSTL is so important that it is hardly exaggerating to call it the essence of Shijo. In this regard, the 5-line format supporters are on good footing. The six-line format is also agreeable.

Displaying in the 7-line format, FSTL displayed as a lone segment of a separate independent line, brings a lot more burden to the writer and the translator, because the reason for the separate display of FSTL should be well served. Unless it is both independent from and connected to the following line, the separate display turns out to be a meaningless effort. Hence, the separate display of FSTL calls for both independence and dependence.

Even Corean Shijo does not carry this burden. It does not display the FSTL in a separate line. Then, in this regard, the English Shijo is under greater restriction than Corean Shijo. But FSTLs in English Shijo don't have to be in 3 syllables, hence the balance is maintained.

Grammar vs Cadence

With the composition of this book, the problem of English grammar surfaced. Rhythm and cadence is the essence of Shijo without which, there can be no Shijo. But still, it is written in a language, which, without grammar does not exist. Here there may well arise some conflict between the grammar and the Shijo cadence. As we have seen above, the famous Shijo poet Yi Ho-woo wrote a 4-syllable word into 3-syllable, for the cadential consideration.

Here are some examples that we faced. We adopted as below:

(A) You tell me what was love like.
(B) Don't be looking only your steps.

But grammatically correct version should be:

(A) You tell me what love was like.
(B) Don't be looking only at your steps.

In (A) and (B), as the grammatically correct version does not sound as rhythmic and cadential, we were forced to adopt the less grammatical ones. But the less grammatical phrases appear in this book only very rarely.

Rhyming

Most Corean Shijo, old or modern, are not rhymed, rather they are, we may say, cadenced and rhythmed. English poetry seems to emphasize rhyming. Unlike English language, Corean language is somewhat rhyme resistant. This is one of the reasons that Shijo and Karsar has grown in Corean language, being rhymed in terms of syllable count, in other words, cadence.

The issue of rhyming matters when it comes to writing English Shijo or translating into English Shijo. I guess "natural" is the answer. Rhyming makes sense only when it sounds more beautiful. As the English language seems to be more rhyme-friendly, English Shijo need not resist rhyming. Rhyming can be an option in English Shijo. Y.T. Byun published rhymed version of Shijo translation in 1948, titled, "Songs From Korea". In this book, some translated Shijo are rhymed in part or in the whole three Lines, but not many.

Arrangement in one Shijo

As we noted before, the display format can vary according to the taste of the writer and we strongly assert that our 7-line format is a good option and that FSTL should be displayed separately. After the display of the line, comes the arrangement. Though we arranged in the manner being shown in this book, other arrangements will also be possible. In this book, the modern Shijo are arranged mostly in the way originally done in the source material.

Afterword

I'd like to make sure that I am not a professional literature scholar, that I haven't read all the materials written by above mentioned authors, and that their opinions quoted here by me, may be different from their true opinions.

Notes

** Below the English translation of Shijo comes the translator's name and below the Corean original, the original writer's name.

** If the original writer's dates of birth and death are not known, it is not marked.

** If the writer's name is not marked, the author is anonymous.

** Shijo are arranged in the order of the Corean alphabet of the original writer's family name. The order is as follows:

K, N, D, R, M, B, S, Y, J, CH, T, P, H.

Part 1: Old Shijo

You water, where are you going?
My way to go, still far away so
I'm flowing on, in pulses
filling up, all the world.
I never stop,
on and on and on
until I reach, the great ocean.

Park Jae Woo

When's it gone, the good old days?
When's it grown, this white hair?
If I'd known, they come through where
Could I have, stopped their ways?
Oh lamenting!
should be the only thing
that I can be, possibly doing.

Lee Kyung-hoon

물아 어디 가느냐
갈 길 멀었어라
뉘 누리 다 채와
지내노라 여흘여흘
창해에
못 미칠 전이야
그칠 줄이 있으랴.

Karng Eek (1523 ~ 1567)

청춘은 언제 가고
백발은 언제 온고
오고 가는 길을
아돗던들 맛을 낫다
알고도
못 막을 길히니
그를 슬허하노라.

Kye Serm

If I hate you, in your presence,
if you are forgotten, when not seen
if you were, never born,
if I didn't, know you at all.....
I'd rather,
vanish away in advance
to make you miss me, as I do miss you.

Park Jae Woo

To seek after, liquor and women,
it should be, none of a poet's business,
to look for, riches and honors,
my heart wouldn't, let me there.
Let it be,
I'd rather be a fisherman or a shepherd,
to be idle and get old, in the peaceful waterside.

Han Jae Eun

보거든 슬믜거나
못 보거든 잊히거나
네 나지 말거나
내 너를 모르거나
차라리
내 먼저 스러져
네 그리게 하리라.

Ko Gyerng-myerng (1533 ~ 1592)

주색 좇자 하니
소인(騷人)의 일 아니고
부귀 구(求)차 하니
뜻이 아니 가네
두어라
어목(漁牧)이 되오야
적막빈(寂寞濱)에 늙자.

Kwern Ho-moon (1533 ~ 1587)

To amuse myself, in rivers and lakes,
is to go against, my gracious lord,
to serve my, gracious lord,
is to get away, from the pleasures.
Standing alone,
at the crossroad at a turning point,
I do not know, which way to take.

Han Jae Eun

All the paths, that the sages took,
at all ages, can't be different.
With a seat, or without a seat,
can it be, ever so different?
When it's same,
then what matters if I
should be staying, at whichever place.

Han Jae Eun

강호에 놀자 하니
성주(聖主)를 버리례고
성주를 섬기자 하니
소락(所樂)에 어기어라.
호온자
기로(岐路)에 서서
갈 데 몰라 하노라.

Kwern Ho-moon (1533 ~ 1587)

성현(聖賢)의 가신 길이
만고에 한가지라.
은(隱)커나 현(見)커나
도(道) 어찌 다르리
일도(一道)오
다르지 아니커니
아무덴들 어떠리.

Kwern Ho-moon (1533 ~ 1587)

You take all, the great fame of yours,
and to be a hero, is not my way either.
When the door's closed, I am in a deep mountain,
when the book's oened, teachers and companions.
Though uncalled for,
by anybody to anywhere,
when joys are done, I shall be leaving.

Han Jae Eun

On a single horse, I came back
to the capital, of five hundred years.
Mountains and streams, are not changed,
where are those, big guys gone?
How sad is it,
that the good peaceful era
only feels like, castles in the air!

Han Jae Eun

공명(功名)도 너 하여라,
호걸(豪傑)도 나 스르어
문 닫으니 심산(深山)이오
책 펴니 사우(師友)로다
오라는
데 없건마는
흥(興) 다 하면 갈가 하노라.

Kee Jerng-jeen (1798 ~ 1879)

오백년 도읍지를
필마(匹馬)로 도라드니
산천(山川)은 의구(依舊)하되
인걸(人傑)은 간 듸 업다.
어즈버
태평연월(太平烟月)이
꿈이런가 하노라.

Keel Jay (1353 ~ 1419)

All sweet sceneries, are given to me
so I've taken them, whole heartedly.
Who would dare, lay his claim
as I alone, am the owner?
Should I ever,
be scowled upon by others,
never do I mean, to share them at all.

Lee Jeong Eun

When the dog, barked at the gate,
I hurried myself, out of the house.
Oh it wasn't my Neem, but the moon full on the lawn,
it's only the sound, from falling leaves.
You dog there,
how'd I know that it was you,
barking sillily at the leaves, falling in the wind?

i

Park Jae Woo

강산 한아(閑雅)한 풍경
다 주어 맞다이셔
내 혼자 님자여니
뉘라셔 다툴소니
남이야
숨꾸지 너긴들
나눠볼 줄 이시랴.

Kim Kwarng-wook (1580 ~ 1656)

시비(柴扉)에 개 짖거늘
님만 여겨 나가 보니
님은 아니 오고 명월이 만정한데
일진추풍(一陣秋風)에 잎지는 소리로다.
저 개야
추풍낙엽을 헛되이 짖어
날 속일 줄 어찌오.

Kim Kwarng-wook (1580 ~ 1656)

Tay san is high, that's what they say
but only a mountain, under the sky.
Har hay is deep, that's what they argue
but a mere, body of water.
High and deep,
should be only the grace
from dear lord, my dear lord.

Park Jae Woo

As the spring mountain, is on fire
the fire spreads, on the blooming flowers.
The fire, on that mountain
has some water, to put it out with
The fire in me,
burning without any smoke inside,
I lament there's no water, that will put it out.

Han Jae Eun

태산(泰山)이 높다 하여도
하늘 아래 뫼이로다.
하해(河海) 깊다 하여도
땅 위에 물이로다.
아마도
높고 깊을 손
성은(聖恩)인가 하노라.

Kim Koo (1488 ~ 1534)

춘산에 불이 나니
못다 핀 꽃 다 붙는다.
저 뫼 저 불은
끌 물이나 있거니와
이 몸에
내 없는 불이 나니
끌 물 없어 하노라.

Kim Derk-ryerng (1567 ~ 1596)

Let my essence, mixed in shool
to flow through, into my lover,
to find every little, piece of my mind
inside his winding guts, nine times folded.
Thereby I could,
wipe out this silly feelings for him
astray from myself, ever facing my love.

ii

Lee Jeong Eun

Love is a lie, it surely is a lie.
Your love for me, is also a lie.
It was a bigger lie, the promise
that you'll see me, in a dream.
Insomniac as I am,
how can you be seen to me,
and where can I, ever be seeing you?

Park Jae Woo

내 정령(精靈) 술에 섞어
님의 속에 흘러들어
구회간장(九回肝腸)을
다 찾아 다닐 망정
날 잊고
남 향한 마음을
다 스로려 하노라

Kim Sarm-hyern

사랑이 거짓말이
님 날 사랑 거짓말이
꿈에 와 뵈단 말이
그 더욱 거짓말이
날같이
잠 아니오면
어늬 꿈에 뵈리오.

Kim Sarng-yong (1561 ~ 1637)

Absent mindedly, attentive to the sound
of the rainfall, touching paulownia leaves,
I hear the rain drops, sound so sad,
maybe as I am, depressed and worried.
From now on,
would I ever plant any trees,
that have big, and wide leaves ?

Han Jae Eun

I am leaving, Sarm gark mountain,
see you again, Han garng waters.
Who'd leave, these mountains
and waters of a dear, mother land.
As it is,
the years of uncertainty and turmoil,
I do wonder, could I see you again?

Park Jae Woo

오동에 듣는 빗발
무심히 듣건마는
내 시름 하니
잎잎이 수성이로다.
이후야
잎 넓은 나무야
심을 줄이 있으랴.

Kim Sarng-yong (1561 ~ 1637)

가노라 삼각산아,
다시 보자 한강수야.
고국 산천을
떠나고자 하랴마는,
시절이
하수상하니,
올동말동 하여라.

Kim Sarng-hern (1570 ~ 1652)

They insist, black is white,
and white, to be black.
Nobody around, black or white,
willed to say, only the truth,
To hear not,
and also to see not,
ears and eyes, I will open not.

Han Jae Eun

The damned hair's, now turned silver,
but my mind's, still fresh ever
when the flowers, are only welcoming,
without seduction, and without flirting,
Oh my wife,
why's it that you scold me,
with that look, that angry look?

Lee Kyung-hoon

검으면 희다하고
희면 검다하네
검거나 희거나
올타하리 전혜(專兮) 업다
찰하로
귀막고 눈감아
듯도 보도 말리라.

Kim Soo-jarng (1690 ~ ?)

터럭은 희었어도
마음은 푸르렀다
꽃은 나를 보고
태(態)없이 반기거늘
각시(閣氏)네
무슨 탓으로
눈 흘김은 엇쩨요

Kim Soo-jarng

Will you please, invite me home,
when home brewed, shool is mature?
I will also, invite you to
my green garden, when It blooms.
Let us talk,
over the means whereby
people can live, free of worries for centuries.

Park Jae Woo

Who are you, looking at me
and saying that, I'm too old?
Still I feel it, like yesterday
when I was, in full vigor.
Whenever,
I see myself in the mirror,
I get struck dumb, not believing my own eyes.

Park Jae Woo

자네 집에 술 익거든
부듸 날 부르시소
초당에 곳 피여든
나도 자네 청하옵세
백년덧
시름 없을 일을
의논코자 하노라.

Kim Yook (1580 ~ 1658)

뉘라셔 날을 보고
늘근이라 하던고
아희 적 하던 일
어제런 듯 하더고나
홀연히
거울곳 보면
나도 어히 없어 하노매라.

Kim Yee-eek (1743 ~ 1830)

The pine tree was cut down recently,
wasn't it the pine, grand and tall?
If it was just left as it was,
wouldn't it have grown to be a good pillar.
My goodness,
if big trees are all cut down,
then which tree will support the tilting country?

Han Jae Eun

Bamboo fenced with well managed pines
this surely is a nice fine bower!
Who would know that I am here,
under the piles of white clouds.
A lone crane,
strolling about the lake slowly,
I declare, is my friend.

iii

Lee Jeong Eun

엊그제 버힌 솔이
낙락장송(落落長松) 아니런가
져근덧 두던들
동량재(棟樑材) 되리러니
어즈버
명당(明當)이 기울면 어느 남기 바티리.

Kim In-hoo (1510 ~ 1560)

대 심어 울을 삼고
솔 가꾸어 정자로다.
백운 덮인 곳에
날 있는 줄 제 뉘 알리.
정반(庭畔)에
학배회(鶴徘徊)하니
그 벗인가 하노라.

Kim Jarng-sayng (1548 ~ 1631)

Sharp wind blows at the top of trees,
the bright moon is chilled on the snow.
I am far away at the front,
on a fort with a sword.
Is there any,
that will dare to stand in my way
at my deep grunt and at my roar.

Lee Jeong Eun

If everybody takes a seat in the office,
whoever there would be a farmer,
If doctors cure all sicknesses,
would Mt. 'Boong marng' be full of the dead?
Dear young lad,
fill the glass to the top,
I'll have the things as I please.

iv

Han Jae Eun

삭풍(朔風)은 나모 긋테 불고
명월(明月)은 눈 속에 찬듸
만리변성(萬里邊城)에
일장검(一長劒) 집고 셔서
긴 파람
큰 한 소릐에
거칠 거시 업세라.

V

Kim Jong-ser (1390 ~ 1453)

벼슬을 저마다 하면
농부 할 이 뉘 있으며
의원이 병 고치면
북망산이 저러하랴.
아해야
잔 가득 부어라
내 뜻대로 하리라.

Kim Chang-erp (1658 ~ 1721)

If the strong should fight for
the scenic beauty of rivers and mountains,
how could I win, even a little,
with my small power and account.
As there are,
no one to forbid me to enjoy,
so I walk around, enjoying the beauty.

Park Jae Woo

Do not hurry, when it's good,
and when it's not, don't take a rest.
Just don't quit, just keep going,
and may you spare every little time!
On the way,
if you quit, then it's not as good
as you had never even started.

Lee Kyung-hoon

강산 죠흔 경을
힘센이 닷톨 양이면,
내 힘과 내 분으로
어이 여 엇들쏜이.
진실로
금 리 업쓸씨
나도 두고 논이노라.

Kim Chern-tayk(18th Century)

잘 가노라 닫지 말며
못 가노라 쉬지 마라
부디 긋지 말고
寸陰(촌음)을 아껴 쓰라
가다가
중지 곳 하면
아니 감만 못하니라.

Kim Chern-tayk

How could I not know that
I may as well be dead any time?
Why am I going on now
laid back now as I am?
It's only that,
I still believe in my lord
that I still expect some bright future.

Park Jae Woo

I climb the Mt. Baykdoo,
holding up the big sword.
I see the world bright below,
pervaded by the cloud of war.
When shall I,
have conquered the war-bearing cloud,
that looms now all over the land.

vi

Lee Kyung-hoon

죽어 옳은 줄을
내거든 모를손가.
물모금 마시고
아무러나 사는 뜻은
늙으신
저 하늘 믿자고
나중 보려 하노라.

Narm Sern (1582 ~ 1654)

장검(長劒)을 빠혀 들고
백두산에 올라 보니
대명천지(大明天地)에
성진(腥塵)이 잠겨세라
언제나
남북풍진(南北風塵)을
헤쳐 볼고 하노라.

General Narm-yi (1441 ~ 1468)

The owl cries in deep sorrow and
the moon sets in the mountain.
Yearning for my far away love,
I rested my head in the pavilion.
Owl, when you cry, my heart always turns into misery.
So if you did not, then my worry would definitely stop.
All the people in the world, who are away from their lovers,
do not dare to come up to this pavilion in spring time,
at night when the moon is bright and the owl is crying.

vii

Han Jae Eun

< Listening to the owl >
A bird in a deep grudge was thrown out of the palace,
mate lost and exiled in the blue forest.
Sleep begged night after night, never coming,
grievance and anger piles every year, never ending.
At the peak now in silence,
only the silver moon gleams bright.
In the spring, the valley is red with fallen flowers.
Heaven should be deaf, or why it never hears,
what this man always hears in deep grievance.

Kim On Seong

촉백제 산월저 하니 상사고 의루두이라.
이제고 아심수 하니 무이성이면 무아수 ㄹ 랏다.
기어인간 이별객 하나니 신막등 춘삼월
자규제 명월루를 하여라.

蜀魄啼 山月低하니 相思苦 倚樓頭라.
爾啼苦 我心愁하니 無爾聲이면 無我愁ㄹ 랏다.
寄語人間 離別客 하나니 愼莫登 春三月
子規啼 明月樓를 하여라.

Boy King Darn-Jong (1441 ~ 1457)

聞子規

端宗

一自寃禽出帝宮
(일자원금출제궁)
孤身隻影碧山中
(고신척영벽산중)
假眠夜夜眠無假
(가면야야면무가)
窮恨年年恨不窮
(궁한년년한불궁)
聲斷曉岑殘月白
(성단효잠잔월백)
血流春谷花落紅
(혈류춘곡화락홍)
天聾尙未聞哀訴
(천롱상미문애소)
胡奈愁人耳獨聽
(호내수인이독청)

< 자규 소리를 듣고 >

한 마리 원한 맺힌 새가 궁중을 나온 뒤로
외로운 몸 짝 없는 그림자 푸른 산 속에 있어
밤마다 잠을 청하건만 잠은 오지 않고
해마다 어렵고 한스럽지만, 한은 다하지 않네.
소리 끊어진 새벽봉우리엔 기울어가는 달만 밝고.
피 뿌린 듯 봄 골짜기에 지는 꽃만 붉구나.
하늘은 귀머거리인가 슬픈 하소연 어이 못 듣고
어찌 수심 많은 이 사람의 귀만 홀로 듣는가.

Boy King Darn-Jong

Though they say that love seen in dreams
cannot be realized to be mine,
where can I ever meet him
when I miss him this so much?
Dear dearest,
just visit me any time
for I'll be happy even in dreams.

Kim On Seong

The sun's now already set,
and I've long, long to go,
Thousands of miles before me
and it's already getting dark.
Fall down,
as I may on the way
will I stop the journey I started?

Lee Kyung-hoon

꿈에 뵈는 님이
신의(信義)업다 하건마는
탐탐(貪貪)이 그리올 제
꿈 아니면 어이보리
져 님아
꿈이라 말고
자로자로 뵈시쇼.

Myerng Ock

날은 저물고
갈 길은 멀었어라.
천리 만리
어스름 하건마는
가다가
엎어진들
가던 길을 말리야.

Park Woon (1493 ~ 1562)

A common sense, this surely is.
On the mirror, when dust gathers,
child or adult, even with a cost
they surely do clean and polish.
Why is it,
that they will never try
to polish their mind without any cost

Lee Kyung-hoon

Three bodies from one womb,
felt like ever the same body.
Two are still away somewhere
with no sign of coming back.
I only sigh,
day after day waiting
by the door at every dusk.

Lee Jeong Eun

명경에 티 끼거든
값주고 닦을 줄
아이 어른 없이
다 미쳐 알건마는
값없이
닦을 명덕(明德)을
닦을 줄을 모르나다.

Park Yin-ro (1561 ~ 1642)

동기로 세 몸 되어
한 몸 같이 지내다가
두 아운 어데 가서
돌아올 줄 모르는고
날마다
석양 문외에
한숨겨워 하노라.

Park Een-ro (1561~1642)

Do not try to do only for your gains,
what others wouldn't seem to like.
Do not follow after others
if it is just not right.
We shall do,
as we are created to do,
keeping to our very own natures.

Park Jae Woo

Have we passed the Cherng serk ridge?
Where is the Cho har goo stream?
The barbaric wind is cold as ice
and worse is the rain that pours on us.
Let someone,
draw my shabbiness and send it
to our lord, away far away.

Park Jae Woo

내해 좋다 하고
남 싫은 일 하지 말며
남이 한다 하고
의 아녀든 좇지 마라
우리는
천성을 지키어
생긴 대로 하리라

Byern Gye-ryang (1369 ~ 1430)

청석령(靑石嶺) 지나거다
초하구(草河溝) 어디메뇨.
호풍(胡風)도 참도찰샤
궂은비는 무슨 일고.
뉘라서
내 행색(行色) 그려내어
님 계신데 드릴고.

Prince Bong-reem
(later, King Hyo jong. 1619～1659. reigned 1649～1659)

You mind there, how could you be
always young and never get old?
When I get old, do you think
you will not be getting old, too?
I fear most,
that I may end up making people laugh
by following you to where you go.

viii

Park Jae Woo

Silly mind makes all silly,
no matter what I would do.
Not even one will be coming
to this mountain beyond clouds.
Dumb as I am,
I would always take it for her
Whenever winds blow leaves about.

Lee Jeong Eun

마음아 너는 어이
매양에 져멋는다.
내 늘글 적이면
넨들 아니 늘글소냐
아마도
너 좃녀 단니다가
남 우일가 하노라.

Ser Kyerng-derk (1489 - 1546)

마음이 어린 후(後) ㅣ 니
하는 일이 다 어리다.
만중운산(萬重雲山)에
어늬 님 오리마난
지난 닙
부난 바람에
행혀 긘가 하노라.

Ser Kyerng-derk

When I've pulled this mountain down,
and filled up that ocean there,
I could walk across the ocean,
to see you at Mt. Bong-nay.
But I am,
like the small-girl-turned bird that longed to see her father,
I wander about before the sea, longing, only longing.

Park Jae Woo

He comes then, he is leaving.
Once he goes, never comes back.
He will just come and go
so can I never see him near
This very day,
He is leaving again,
letting me down, into sadness.

Lee Kyung-hoon

이 뫼를 헐어내어
저 바다를 메우면은
봉래산(蓬萊山) 고운 님을
걸어가도 보련마는
이 몸이
정위조(精衛鳥) 같아야
바자닐만 하노라.

Ser Yik (1542 ~ 1587)

오면 가려 하고
가면 아니 오네.
오노라 가노라니
볼 날이 전혀 없네.
오늘도
가노라 하니
그를 슬퍼하노라.

King Sern jo (1552 ~ 1608. reigned 1567 ~ 1608)

What shall I be after I die,
after my flesh'n bone is buried?
First a tall pine tree rising
at the peak of Mt. Bong nay.
Then I'll be,
standing fresh and green alone,
when heaven'n earth's buried in the snow.

Han Jae Eun

In the field spring's returned,
and this body gets so busy.
Who is to move the flowering trees,
when to finish plowing the field?
Bring me over,
some bamboo trees I will
be weaving a hat conic first.

Lee Kyung-hoon

이 몸이 죽어가서
무엇이 될꼬 하니
봉래산 제일봉에
낙낙장송 되어 있어
백설이
만건곤할 제
독야청청 하리라.

Serng Sarm moon (1418 ~ 1456)

전원(田園)에 봄이 오니
이 몸이 일이 하다
꽃 남근 뉘 옴기며
약(藥)밧츤 언제 갈리
아희야,
대 뷔여 오나라
삿갓 몬져 겨르리라.

Serng Hon (1535 ~ 1598)

Green hills without words,
flowing water without form,
fresh wind free of charge,
bright moon without owner.
Amidst these,
let this body with no illness
get old with no judgement of good and bad.

Lee Jeong Eun

I ask you Myerng na river,
tell us how Gool wern died.
As there is nowhere to bury
this very body, slandered body,
I will wash,
all my bones in the water
to bury them inside fish.

ix

Lee Kyung-hoon

말 업슨 청산(靑山)이요
태(態) 업슨 유수(流水) ㅣ 로다
갑 업슨 청풍(靑風)이요,
님자 업슨 명월(明月)이라.
이 중(中)에
병(病) 업슨 이 몸이
분별(分別) 업시 늙으리라.

Serng Hon

묻노라 멱라수(汨羅水)
굴원(屈原)이 어찌 죽다터니
참소(讒訴)에 더럽힌
몸 묻힐 땅이 없어
창파(滄波)에
골곡(骨曲)을 씻어
어복리(漁腹裏)에 장(葬)하리라.

Serng Choong (? - 656)

On a day of wind and frost,
the lord sent in some golden chrysanthemums
freshly bloomed, in a golden vase,
to us in the "Hall of Academia'.
Peach or plum,
don't you ever pretend to be flowers
as I guess I see what He means for us.

Park Jae Woo

With my mind, I talked about
retiring away 'cause we are too old.
The mind said, "Where could I wish to go?
Why would I want to leave this man behind?"
Dear mind,
just stay with that man,
this body will be leaving away first.

Park Jae Woo

풍상(風霜)이 섞어 친 날에
갓 피온 황국화(黃菊花)를
금분(金盆)에 가득 담아
옥당(玉堂)에 보내오니
도리(桃李)야
꽃이온 양 마라
님의 뜻을 알괘라.

Song Soon (1493 ~ 1582)

늙었다 물러가자
마음과 의논하니
이 님 버리고
어드러로 가잔 말고.
마음아
너란 있거라
몸만 먼저 가리라.

Song Soon

Ten years of hard work
has achieved this small cottage.
A room for me, another for the moon
and another for the cool breeze.
Not a room,
for streams and hills,
so I will be looking around.

Lee Jeong Eun

You need not be sad at
the falling flowers, birds there.
They did not fall by themselves
but by the wind, blowing hard.
Now I see,
envying the spring should count for little,
as it's happy to leave, shedding down the flowers.

Lee Jeong Eun

십년을 경영(經營)하여
초려삼간(草廬三間) 지어내니
나 한 칸 달 한 칸에
청풍(淸風) 한간 맡겨두고
강산(江山)은
들일 데 없으니
둘러두고 보리라.

Song Soon

꽃이 진다 하고
새들아 슬퍼마라.
바람에 흩날리니
꽃의 탓 아니로다.
가노라
희짓는 봄을
새워 무슴하리오.

Song Soon

When I said that my name was pine,
what kind of pine did you think it was?
The great tall one on the deep steep cliff,
that sure is what I am.
A small sickle,
of a young shepherd down the road,
will never be hanging on my boughs.

x

Park Jae Woo

You tell me what was love like.
Was it round, or was it square?
Was it long, or was it short?
To be measured by a foot or by a scale?
I don't know,
If I can say it was very long,
but I do not know where its tip falls.

Han Jae Eun

솔이 솔이라 하니
무슨 솔만 너겻난다
천심절벽(千尋絶壁)의
낙락장송(落落長松) 내 긔로다
길 아릐
초동(樵童)의 졉낫시야
거러 볼 줄이 이시랴.

Song Yee

사랑이 엇떠터니
둥고더냐 모지더냐
길더냐 져르더냐
발일넌냐 자힐너냐
각별이
긴 줄은 모로되
끝 간 듸를 몰내라.

Song Yee

I immediately forget what I heard,
I pretend to have never seen.
This being the way I live in the world.
I don't know the rights or wrongs of others.
Only my hand,
remaining sound so I am
just grabbing the cup, only the cup.

Kim On Seong

I was a child who would laugh
at those men with white hair.
I never knew some other day
other children would laugh at me.
Little children,
you do not laugh at me,
as I was that laughing child.

Lee Kyung-hoon

들은 말 즉시 잊고
본 일도 못 본 듯이
내 人事 이러호매
남의 是非 모를로다.
다만지
손이 성하니
잔 잡기만 하노라.

Song Yeen (1517 ~ 1584)

아해 제 늘그니 보고
백발(白髮)을 비웃더니
그 더듸 아해들이
날 우슬 줄 어이 알리.
아해야
하 웃지 마라
나도 웃던 아해로다.

Sheen Gye-yerng (1577 ~ 1669)

Look, children, don't you be
too happy for the advance of New Years.
Hectic days and years will
take away the young child.
Ourselves too,
welcoming the new years,
got us this hair, snow white hair.

Han Jae Eun

Had someone who made songs
had sorrows himself as much?
Maybe he couldn't say enough,
that he tried to sing them off.
If it does,
if it really will work it off,
then I'd sing off anguishes of mine, too.

Park Jae Woo

이봐 아이들아
새해 온다 즐겨마라.
헌사한 세월이
소년 앗아 가느니라.
우리도
새해 즐겨하다가
이 백발이 되었노라.

Shin Gye-yerng

노래 삼긴 사람
시름도 하도 할샤
일러 다 못 일러
불러나 푸돗던가
진실로
풀릴 것이면
나도 불러 보리라.

Sheen Hum (1566 ~ 1628)

What's the heron about to do,
standing long on the river?
Why would you keep watching there
the fish swimming absently about?
Let it be,
When you two share the water,
what is the point of keeping watch?

xi

Park Jae Woo

The Great Mountain, they say is so steep,
but it's only a mountain under the sky.
If one climbs up and up,
no one will ever fail to the top.
But he only
would say around that it's too high
for him to climb when he never tried enough.

xii

Park Jae Woo

냇가에 해오라비
무슨 일로 서 있는가
무신한 저 고기를
여어 무엇 하려는가
두어라
한 물에 있으니
여어 무엇 하리오.

Sheen Hum

태산이 높다 하되
하늘 아래 뫼이로다.
오르고 또 오르면
못 오를 리 없건마는
사람이
제 아니 오르고
뫼만 높다 하더라.

Yarng Sar-ern (1517 ~ 1584)

All the mountains are my side dish.
I will brew shool from pure ocean water.
Singing insane songs,
mourning the past thousand years,
I will not go back until I get drunk.

Kim On Seong

Having left my fair lord,
far away and far apart,
I sat alone at a stream,
'cause I had nowhere to put my heart.
The water there,
must be like my heart walking
along the dark path, sobbing only sobbing.

xiii

Kim On Seong

< 불취원무귀(不醉願無歸) >

山岳爲肴核(산악위효핵)　높고 낮은 산을 안주로 삼고,
滄溟作酒池(창명작주지)　푸른 바다 물로 술을 빚어.
狂歌凋萬古(광가조만고)　미친 노래 불러 만고를 슬퍼하면서,
不醉願無歸(불취원무귀)　취하지 않으면 돌아가지 않으리.

Yarng Sar-ern (1517 ~ 1584)

천만리 머나먼 길에
고운 님 여의옵고
내 마음 둘 데 없어
냇가에 앉았으니
저 물도
내 안 같아여
울어 밤길 예놋다.

Warng Barng-yern

The king asked for a response to his song;

You crow, don't be black,
white heron, don't be white.
Blacks and whites are so dizzying.
You eagle,
how could you be
neither black, nor white?

Lee Yarng wern answered,

What is red is not me,
nor am I what is blue.
Beauty of red or blue
being not even close to me,
then why would you say,
that I've got colored,
not knowing who I really am?

Park Jae Woo

왕이 다음과 같이 노래 불러 화답을 청하였다…

까마귀야 검지 말라,
백로야 희지 말라.
흑백이 어지럽다.
수리야 너는 어찌
검지도 희지도 않느냐?

이양원이 대답하였다…

붉다 하여도 내 아니요,
푸르다 하여도 내 아니라,
붉고 푸름의 눈부심도
내 고움이 아니거늘
님은 어찌하여
날 몰라보고
물들었다 하시오?

Lee Yarng-wern (1533 ~ 1592)

< Traces of the Old Castle >

When the night falls on there,
only the moonlight looms silent.
It tries to tell the story to me
about the ruins of the castle.

Ah ~ a lonely roamer there,
unable to sleep alone and sad
at the unceasing sounds of bugs,
he just lets the tears flow down.

The castle's demolished to be empty,
only grass is fine as green,
suggesting the vanity of this world.

Ah ~ What a poor thing, really am I,
kicking about aimlessly to search,
on the dreamy road for something.

I'm now willed to go, without stopping
wherever my step'll lead me to,
over the mountains across the oceans,
with no destination in mind.

Ah ~ this grief, never ending,
I hold it deep in my chest.
Farewell, you old castle,
as I must be flowing away first.

xiv

Park Jae Woo

< 황성옛터 > (옛이름: 황성의 적(跡))

황성옛터에 밤이 되니 월색만 고요해
페허에 서린 회포를 말하여 주노나
아 ~ 외로운 저 나그네 홀로이 잠못 이뤄
구슬픈 벌레소리에 말없이 눈물져요

성은 허물어져 빈터인데 방초만 푸르러
세상이 허무한 것을 말하여 주노나
아 ~ 가엾다 이 내몸은 그 무엇 찾으려
덧없는 꿈의 거리를 헤매여 있노라

나는 가리로다 끝이 없이 이 발길 닿는 곳
산을 넘고 물을 건너 정처가 없이도
아 ~ 한없는 이 서름을 가슴속 깊이 안고
이 몸은 흘러서 가노니 옛터야 잘 있거라.

Warng Pyerng (1908 ~ 1941)

Wind melted the snow on the mountains
and suddenly blew out of my sight.
I will borrow it for a few minutes
to have it blow over my head.
I dare wish,
to melt away these old frosts
aged long by the ears.

XV

Lee Jeong Eun

I willed not to get old
I did will to get young again.
Yet my youth fooled me around,
most of the hair turned gray already.
It's no use,
that I try not to feel guilty
whenever I walk by the flower bed.

Lee Jeong Eun

청산에 눈 녹인 바람
건 듯 불고 간 데 없다
적은 덧 빌어다가
머리 위에 불리고저
귀밑에
해묵은 서리를
녹여볼까 하노라.

Woo Tark (1263~1342)

늙지 말려 하고
다시 젊어 보렸더니
청춘이 날 속이고
백발이 거의로다.
이따금
꽃밭을 지날 때면
죄 지은 듯 하여라.

Woo Tark

With a good stick in one hand,
with a sharp thorn in the other,
I tried with the thorn, to stop the aging,
to hit with the stick the white hair coming.
Then the snowy hair,
knowing all these in advance,
came to me through the shortcut.

Han Jae Eun

Who dares to call the bamboo,
bent down by the snow as crooked?
If it was intended to bend itself,
Can it be staying green in the snow?
I declare,
It is you dear, the one and only,
who can bear through harshest winters.

Lee Jeong Eun

한 손에 막대잡고
또 한손에 가시쥐고
늙는 길 가시로 막고
오는 백발 막대기로 치려터니
백발이
제 몬저 알고
즈렴길로 오더라 .

Woo Tark

눈 마자 휘어진 대를
뉘라셔 굽다탄고.
구블 절(節)이면
눈 속에 프를소냐.
아마도
세한고절(歲寒高節)은
너뿐인가 하노라.

Wern Chern-serk (1330 ~ ?)

Ups and downs meant to be,
Amid dust is the Grand Palace now.
Half millennium kingdom's now
on a piece of a herder's flute.
A wanderer,
passing under the setting sun
only takes steps in the tears.

xvi

Lee Jeong Eun

The stream that cried along last night
flowed by me crying sadly.
Now I know it was you
who sent me these sad waters.
I'd cry aloud
to make it flow back up,
to reach you at your place.

Park Jae Woo

흥망이 유수하니
만월대도 추초로다
오백년 왕업이
목적에 부쳤으니
석양에
지나는 객이
눈물겨워 하노라.

Wern Chern-serk

간 밤의 우뎐 여흘
슬피 우러 지내여다.
이제아 생각하니
님이 우러 보내도다.
져 물이
거스리 흐르고져
나도 우러 녜리라.

Wern Ho (1397 ~ 1463)

As the night comes along,
autumn river runs cold by.
I threw the line in the water,
but not one would come by.
I go back,
only paddling back the empty boat,
loaded with the moon that only shines.

xvii

Kim On Seong

추강(秋江)에 밤이 드니
물결이 차노매라
낙시 드리치니
고기 아니 무노매라.
無心(무심)한
달빛만 싣고
빈 배 저어 오노라.

Prince Werl-sarn (1454 ~ 1488)

This Shijo is the translation of Chinese poem by 冶父道川, the zen master during Song China.

千尺絲綸直下垂
I dropped a line of ten thousand feet
一波纔動萬波隨
A wave rises causing many other waves
夜靜水寒魚不食
Silent night, water's cold, fish wouldn't bite
滿船空載月明歸
I come back, boat loaded with moonshine.

All night last night, the wind blew hard.
Blew so hard, with snows and frosts.
Tall hanging pines hundred years old
are now all tilting down.
Then, what more
is needed to ask about
the flowers yet to bloom.

Lee Kyung-hoon

No visitors come by and,
fallen leaves pile out the door.
Long bamboo out the window,
casts a patch of green shade.
With the incense alight,
and sitting all day alone in the quiet study,
holding in hand a potery book,
I recite T'ang poems alone.

Han Jae Eun

간밤의 부던 바람에
눈 서리 치단 말가.
낙락장송이
다 기우러 가노매라
하믈며
못다 핀 곳이야
닐러 므슴 하리오.

Yoo Ung-boo (? ~ 1456)

문밖엔 찾아오는 이 없어
낙엽만 가득 쌓였고
창밖엔 기다란 대나무가
푸르스름 그늘을 드리웠네.
한가로운 서재에서
하루종일 향을 피우고 앉아서
손에 唐詩를 잡고
나혼자 읊어보네.

Yoo Hee-gyerng (1545 ~ 1636)

< Dedicated to Kye'rarng >

Look, I have a miraculous medicine
that can cure even frowns on a pretty face.
I will hold it in secret,
wrapping it up in my silk pocket.
and will give it to my love
when I meet one someday.

xviii

Kim On Seong

Silver dew falls from the autumn sky,
and cinnamon flowers bloomed in full.
I snapped the loftiest twig in hand,
and came back accompanied by the bright moon.

Han Jae Eun

< 증계랑(贈癸娘) > - 계랑에게 주다
나에게 선약(仙藥)이 하나 있는데
고운 얼굴 찡그린 것을 고칠 수도 있다네.
비단 주머니에 감추어 두었다가
정다운 사람 생기면 나누어주고 싶어라.

Yoo Hee-gyerng

가을 하늘에서 흰 이슬이 내려
산속에 계수나무 꽃이 활짝 피었네
가장 높은 가지를 꺾어들고서
밝은 달을 벗삼아 돌아왔다네.

Yoo Hee-gyerng

You are in Boo arn, I am in Seoul.
so we cannot see each other,
when we long so much for each other.
Whenever rain falls on the paulownia leaves,
I feel my bowels just get cut.

Han Jae Eun

< First impression on May charng >
The name Kye rarng has resounded already
for her writings and singing talents.
Now I've met her in person at last
I see a goddess come down from up above.

Kim On Seong

娘家在浪州　그대의 집은 부안에 있고
我家住京口　나의 집은 서울에 있어
相思不相見　그리움 사무쳐도 서로 못보고
腸斷梧桐雨　오동나무에 비뿌릴 젠 애가 끊겨라.

Yoo Hee-gyerng

曾聞南國癸娘名　남국의 계랑 이름 일찍이 알려져서
詩韻歌詞動洛城　글 재주 노래 솜씨 서울에까지 울렸어라
今日相看眞面目　오늘에사 참모습을 대하고 보니
却疑神女下三淸　선녀가 떨쳐입고 내려온 듯하여라

Yoo Hee-gyerng

< Moon Streamed Path >

The mountain's misty with the scent of rain,
and fog starts to rise on the water.
A heron dozes near the Lake Pure,
the path curves down by the sweetbriers
and snow falls on the whip from the twigs.

Kim On Seong

Only with a cup in the hand
I am seeing the distant mountain.
The pleasure of her coming back
could it ever be as good as this?
Though it is,
with no words and with no smiles,
I cannot but love the mountain.

Park Jae Woo

< 月溪途中 >

山含雨氣水生烟　산은 빗기운 머금고 물엔 안개 피어나
青草湖邊白鷺眠　청초호 물가에선 백로가 조은다.
路入海棠花下轉　해당화 아래쪽으로 길은 꺾어들고,
滿枝香雪落揮鞭　가지 가득 얹힌 눈은 채찍 끝에 떨어지네.

Yoo Hee-gyerng

잔 들고 혼자 안자
먼 뫼흘 바라보니
그리던 님이 오다
반가옴이 이러하랴
말삼도
웃움도 아녀도
몯내 됴하 하노라.

Yoon Sern-do (1587 ~ 1671)

'Five Friends' by Yoon Sern do

xix

< prelude >
Who are the dearest friends of mine?
Water, Rock, Pine and Bamboo.
As moon rises above the hill,
more pleasure comes to me.
What more else,
would I desire when I have
these five dear friends of mine?

Kim On Seong

< Rock >
What makes flowers fall so early,
so soon after they are bloomed?
What makes grass turn so yellow,
from the moment they are green?
Perhaps the rock
is the only thing
that will never change itself.

Lee Kyung-hoon

오우가(五友歌)

< 전체 >

내 버디 몇이나 하니
수석(水石)과 송죽(松竹)이라.
동산에 달 오르니
긔 더욱 반갑고야
두어라
이 다섯 밖에
또 더하여 머엇 하리.

< 바위 >

고즌 므스 일로
퓌며셔 쉬이 디고
플은 어이 하야
프르는 듯 누르나니
아마도
변티 아닐손
바회 뿐인가 하노라.

< Pine >

Flowers bloom when it's warm,
Leaves will fall when it's cold.
My dear pine, how is it
that you never know snow or frost.
Who wouldn't know
that you are rooted deep down
deep down even to the underworld.

Lee Kyung-hoon

< Water >

The clouds above command a view,
but turn dark whenever they please.
the clear sounds of the wind
often do not stay by me.
I declare,
it sure is only the water
that is clean and stays on.

Lee Kyung-hoon

< 소나무 >

더우면 곳 퓌고
치우면 닙 디거늘
솔아 너는 얻디
눈 서리를 모르는다.
구천(九泉)의
불희 고든 줄을
글로하야 아노라.

< 물 >

구름 빗치 조타 하나
검기를 자로 한다.
바람 소리 맑다 하나
그칠 적이 하노매라.
조코도
그츨 뉘 업기는
믈 뿐인가 하노라.

< Bamboo >

It is not one of the trees,
nor is it a sort of grass.
With the most straight body
how could it empty itself?
As it bears,
the color of green all the season,
who can ever resist loving it?

Park Jae Woo

< Moon >

High in the sky, a tiny material
shedding lights down on the world.
Is there any that is as bright
as you are in the night.
You see all,
without saying anything,
I guess you are my dear friend.

Lee Kyung-hoon

< 竹 >

나모도 아닌 거시
플도 아닌 거시,
곳기는 뉘 시기며
속은 어이 뷔연는다.
뎌러코
사시예 프르니
그를 됴햐 하노라.

< 月 >

쟈근 거시 노피 떠셔
만물을 다 비취니
밤듕의 광월(光月)이
너만 하니 또 잇느냐.
보고도
말 아니하니
내 벋인가 하노라.

Have we passed the cold winter?
Where's it gone, the biting blizzard?
I see spirits of coming spring
on the mountains and the hills.
At dawn,
opening the mountain wicket,
I will be looking at the shade of the sky.

Lee Jeong Eun

The candlelight in the room,
who did it break up with?
Shedding tears on the outside
burning itself, on the inside.
We may be,
the same as the candle,
we don't know we are burning.

xx

Lee Kyung-hoon

엄동이 지나거냐
설풍(雪風)이 어디 가니
천산만산에
봄기운이 어리었다.
지게를
신조(晨朝)에 열고서
하늘빛을 보리라.

Yoon Sern-do

방 안에 혓난 촛불
눌과 이별 하였관대
겉으로 눈물 지고
속 타는 줄 모르는고
우리도
저 촛불 갓하야
속 타는 줄 모르노라.

Yi Kay (1417 ~ 1456)

Can this be always right and
can that be always wrong?
Will this fight end some day,
when the two sides are only the same?
If the lord,
should work as the just scale to judge by,
then I guess the fight will end by itself.

Park Jae Woo

They fight everyday with all might,
is it for, for our country?
With enough food, and enough clothes,
they will do nothing other than fighting.
If they never,
stop the fighting they started,
what should be done, what can we do?

Kim On Seong

이라 다 옳으며
제라 다 그르랴.
두편이 같아서
이 싸움 아니 마네.
성군이
준칙(準則)이 되시면
절로 말까 하노라.

Yi Derk-il

힘써 하는 싸움
나라 위한 싸움인가.
옷밥에 묻혀 있어
할 일 없어 싸우놋다.
아마도
그치지 아니하니
다시 어이하리.

Yi Derk-il

I will catch a wild goose and win it over
with my true heart, and tame it.
I will teach the way to my Neem's home,
as vividly as it will never forget.
Then whenever,
I miss him at midnight,
I will have it bring my words to him.

Han Jae Eun

< Lament >
On a frosty spring day,
I was sewing winter clothes.
The sunlight was coming in
through the silk window.
Then suddenly,
face buried in my hands,
Tears fell down
soaking the needle and thread.

Han Jae Eun

기러기 산 채로 잡아
정들이고 길들여서
님의 집 가는 길을
역력(歷歷)히 가르쳐주고
한밤중
님 생각날 제면
소식 전케 하리라

xxi

Yi May-charng (1513 ~ 1550)

< 自恨 >

春冷補寒衣　차가운 봄날, 겨울 옷을 꿰매는데
紗窓日照時　사창에는 햇빛이 비치고 있네
低頭信手處　머리를 두 손으로 감싸니
珠淚滴針絲　눈물이 구슬처럼 떨어져 실과 바늘을 적시네

Yi May-charng

< Lament for fate >
People are fond of flutes,
but I strum on the ker moon go.
Not until now, did I know,
it's so hard to go my own way.
Like the man, whose feet were cut
and insulted three times,
who tried to meet the true one
his jade belongs to,
today I embrace my lump of jade,
sobbing inward at my Mt. Hyerng.

xxii xxiii

Han Jae Eun

When pear blossoms were falling down,
we parted in the cries and hugs.
Is he also thinking of me
amid the fall of autumn leaves?
The lonely dreams,
will come on and off spanning
the thousand miles between him and me.

Han Jae Eun

< 自恨 薄命 >

사람들은 피리를 좋아하지만
나는 거문고를 타네
세상 길 가기 어려움
오늘에야 비로소 알겠네.
발 잘려 세 번이나 부끄러움
당하고도 임자를 만나지 못해
아직도 옥덩이를 붙안고 형산에서 우노라.

Yi May-charng

이화우(梨花雨) 흩뿌릴 제
울며 잡고 이별한 님
추풍낙엽(秋風落葉)에
저도 날 생각난가.
천 리에
외로운 꿈만
오락가락 하노매.

Yi May-charng

Had my footprints been carved
on the road in my dreams,
the path by the window of my Neem
would've worn out even if it's in rock.
No trace left,
on the road in my sweet dreams,
turns me sad, brings me down.

Lee Jeong Eun

If it's this way, should it matter?
If it's that way, then would it matter?
The hanging vines over'n that Mt. Marnsoo,
are they to blame for the entanglement?
Then why not,
get entangled together,
to be blessed for a hundred years.

xxiv

Lee Kyung-hoon

꿈에 다니는 길이
자취 곳 나랑이면
님의 집 창 밖에
석로라도 닳으련마는
꿈길이
자취 없으니
그를 슬허하노라.

Yi Myerng-harn (1595 ~ 1645)

이런들 어떠하며
저런들 어떠하리
만수산 드렁칡이
얽어진들 어떠하리
우리도
이같이 얽어져
백년까지 누리리라

Yi Barng-wern
(1367 ~ 1422. later the third king Tay-jong
r. 1400 ~ 1418)

< At May-charng's grave >

The gravestone is aged but golden turf is afresh.
Though wind and rain would come and go as ever,
A fistful of this scented earth gets never demolished.
I see her sing the song of the 'pear blossoms',
and putting aside the ker mooon go,
she sits alone by the lamp.
Who is she thinking of now?
Sad tears on the cheek seem to flow down.
How many times must she have torn her clothes by herself?
The love with him ended in vain,
but her longings remain alive to this day,
as is written in the beautiful poetry of hers.

XXV

Han Jae Eun

< 매창뜸 >

돌비는 낡아지고 금잔디 새로워라
덧없이 비와 바람 오고가고 하지마는
한 줌의 향기로운 이 흙 헐리지를 않는다.
이화우 부르다가 거문고 비껴두고
등 아래 홀로 앉아 누구를 생각는지
두 뺨에 젖은 눈물이 흐르는 듯 하구나
羅衫裳(나삼상) 손에 잡혀 몇 번이나 찢었으리
그리던 雲雨도 스러진 꿈이 되고
그 고운 글발 그대로 정은 살아 남았다.

Yi Byeong-gi (1891 ~ 1968)

The dark clouds are now looming
at the vale snow is drying.
Where should it be blooming,
the welcome blossoms of May-hwar?
Stood alone,
in the glow of setting sun,
I wonder where should I turn to.

xxvi

Park Jae Woo

Men gone can't see me
I can not see them either.
Though I can't meet them now
the paths they took lie before me.
Standing as I am,
right before the path they took,
which other path is there for me to take?

Kim On Seong

백설이 잦아진 골에
구름이 머흐레라
반가운 매화는
어느 곳에 피었는고
석양에
홀로 서서
갈 곳 몰라 하노라.

Yi Sayk (1328 ~ 1396)

고인도 날 못 보고
나도 고인 못뵈
고인을 못봐도
예던 길 앞에 있네
예던 길
앞에 있거든
아니 예고 어쩔꼬

Yi Hwarng (1501 ~ 1570)

The monk at the field comes
to me for a piece of poetry.
My neighbor, an aged man
brought along a bottle of shool.
Short hair gets white,
from reciting fine poems,
and aged face flushes up
drunken by the shool.
A cow walks on the watery grass
and birds fly on flower shedding winds.
Maybe I was born with rural taste,
I walk about in sickness.

Lee Jeong Eun

Who would know if my clothes
would be passed abroad.
I clearly recall this saying of Kyu'jay's.
Thereafter prices have all risen up
Yet my lines haven't as much.

xxvii xxviii

Lee Jeong Eun

들판의 스님은 시 지어달라 찾아오고
이웃 노인은 술을 보내와
짧은 머리는 시 읊다가 희어지고
시든 얼굴은 술에 취해 붉어지네
소는 비내린 풀밭을 가고
새는 꽃 떨군 바람 속에 나니
시골 흥취를 아마도 타고 났는지
병 중에 이리저리 거니네.

Yi Sayk (1328 ~ 1396)

누가 알랴, 나의 의발이 해외로 전해질른지
규재의 그 한 말씀이 아직도 또렷한데
그 뒤로 물가가 모두 올랐건만
유독 내 문장만은 돈 값어치가 안 나간다네.

Yi Sayk

< Composed for fun >
The crude poems by this man,
have piled up to the roof,
a little clumsy letter by letter.
But the lines, when I recite,
the purity spreads so very deeply
into the bone often times,
like dew sprinkled in an autumn sky

Kim On Seong

Han san island moony night
sitting alone at a post,
bearing a sword on my side,
I was moaning in a deep sigh.
From somewhere
A reed song apparently Manchurian
its touching tune cuts into my heart.

Lee Jeong Eun

< 장난삼아 짓다 >
목은의 시가 몇 축이나 가득 차
읊어보면 글자 마다 서툴긴 해도
이따금 맑은 정취가 뼛속까지 사무쳐
갠 하늘에 가을 이슬 뿌린 듯 하네.

Yi Sayk

한산(閑山)셤 달 발근 밤의
수루(戍樓)에 혼자 안자
큰 칼 녀픠 차고
기픈 시름 하난 적의
어듸셔
일성호가(一聲胡笳)난
남의 애를 긋나니.

Yi Soon-shin (1545 ~ 1598)

I tried to confess my agonies
in the letter to dear home.
But I imagined my father in white hair
will be worrying about me.
Though snow on a shadowed mountain
has piled up and reached the roof top,
I write that this winter's so warm
that it seems like a spring season.

Kim On Seong

I was offered to climb up
to a very high tree top.
Hey, there, dear friends of mine,
please do not push around this tree.
Falling down,
to the ground to death is not what I fear,
but I fear that I might not be able to see the lord.

Kim On Seong

欲作家書說苦辛　집에 보낼 편지에 괴로움 말하려 해도
恐教愁殺白頭親　흰 머리의 어버이 근심하실까 저어하여
陰山積雪深千丈　그늘진 산, 쌓인 눈이 깊이가 천장인데
却報今冬暖似春　금년 겨울은 봄처럼 따뜻하다 말하네.

Yi Arn-nool (1571 ~ 1637)

높으나 높은 남게
날 권하여 올려두고
이보오 벗님네야
흔들지나 말으되야
나려져
죽기는 섧지 아니되
님 못 볼까 하노라.

Yi Yang-wern (1533 ~ 1592)

I welcome the moon that my lord saw
As much as if I see him here.
Would the lord also welcome you
as if he were seeing me?
I'd rather,
be the moon and shed my light,
on my lord, on my cherished lord.

Kim On Seong

Though sun shines in thousand threads
can it tie down the breeze leaving?
Bees and butterflies, fly about as they may,
would there be a way to do with blossoms falling?
However cherished,
is my love toward him,
What could I do about the Neem leaving?

Lee Jeong Eun

님 보신 달 보고
님 뵈온 듯 반기노라.
님도 너를 보고
날 본 듯 반기는가.
차라리
저 달이 되어서
비추어나 보리라.

Yi Wern-ik (1547 ~ 1634)

녹양(綠楊)이 천만사(千萬絲)인들
가는 춘풍 잡아매며
탐화봉접(探花蜂蝶)인들
지는 꽃을 어이하리.
아무리
사랑이 중한들
가는 님을 어이리.

Yi Wern-ik (1547 ~ 1634)

Is the lord someone that I can trust?
He must be the one I shouldn't trust.
I already knew I couldn't trust him,
even during those years of trust.
Indeed,
it is not difficult to trust him,
but what can I do but trust him first?

Kim On Seong

To retire home has been only empty promise,
Nobody's going back to the countryside.
Every which person would surely know
that rank and fame is like floating clouds.
But no one,
seems to be awake from the dream
so, for which, I feel most sorry.

Kim On Seong

님을 믿을 것가
못믿을 손 님이시라.
믿어 온 시절도
못믿을 줄 알았어라.
믿기야
어려우랴마는
아니 믿고 어이리.

Yi Jerng-gwi (1564 ~ 1635)

歸去來 歸去來 한들
물러간 이 긔 누구며
功名이 浮雲인 줄
사람마다 알건마는
세상에
꿈 깬 이 없으니
그를 슬허하노라.

Yi Jerng-bo

Moon breaks white on pear blossoms
and milky way reaches into midnight.
The night bird, how could it know
the feel of the coming spring hidden in a branch?
I could not,
sleep a wink, even a wink tonight,
as if it were an illness, the sensitivity to me.

xxix

Park Jae Woo

이화에 월백하고
은한이 삼경인 제,
일지춘심을
자규야 알랴마는
다정도
병인 양 하여,
잠 못 들어 하노라.

Yi Jo-nyern (1269 ~ 1343)

한역(漢譯)

梨花月白三更天　(이화월백삼경천)
啼血聲聲怨杜鵑　(제혈성성원두견)
儘覺多情原是病　(진각다정원시병)
不關人事不成眠　(불관인사불성면)

신위(申緯), <경수당전고(警脩堂全藁)>

The famous saying, clouds are innocent,
could it be any more wrong?
Floating high up in the sky,
they will go every which way.
Why on earth,
is it that they will follow
after the sun and cover it?

xxx

Lee Kyung-hoon

Do not laugh, you white heron,
At a crow for its black.
Though black on the skin,
Underneath it cannot be black.
I can tell,
that you are the one for sure,
face white and heart black.

Lee Jeong Eun

구름이 무심탄 말이
아마도 허랑하다.
중천에 떠있어
임의로 다니면서
구태여
광명한 날빛을
따라가며 덮나니.

Yi Jon-o

가마귀 검다 하고
백로야 웃지 마라
겉이 검은들
속조차 검을소냐
겉 희고
속 검은 이는
너뿐인가 하노라.

Yi Jik (1362 ~ 1431)

You cloud there, taking a rest
before flying across the high hill.
How about taking some tears of mine,
the bitter grudged tears of this lonely servant,
to have it,
sprinkled down on the court,
where my lord is, where my dear lord is?

Lee Jeong Eun

I often used to fish here,
when I was a little one.
Thirty years have been lost
into the wind and dust of the world.
I still recognize mountains and rivers,
but don't know if they do me, an old man now.

Kim On Seong

철령 높은 곳에
쉬어넘는 저 구름아
고신원루(孤臣冤淚)를
비삼아 띄워다가
님 계신
구중심처에
뿌려본들 어떠리.

Yi Harng-bok

어린 시절 여기서 낚시했는데
삼십년 세월을 풍진 속에 저버렸네
시내와 산의 얼굴을 나는 알아보지만
시내와 산은 늙은 나를 알아볼지

Yi Hwarng

At the valley, grass is thick
are you sleeping or just lying?
Where's it gone, that ruddy face of yours?
Now is it only bleached bone of yours?
As there is,
no one to share the drink with,
do I feel lonely and melancholy.

Kim On Seong

Heard Northern Sky was now clear,
went the way without a raincoat.
It snows on the mountains,
and rain falls cold on the field.
As I am,
soaked today in the cold rain,
I may as well be sleeping frozen.

xxxi *and look opposite page*

Han Jae Eun

청초 우거진 골에 자난다 누웠난다
홍안은 어디 두고 백골만 묻혔나니
잔 잡아 권할 이 없으니 그를 설어 하노라.

Yim Je (1549 ~ 1587)

북천이 맑다커를 우장 업시 길을 나니
산의는 눈이 오고 들에는 챠비 온다
오늘은 찬비 마자시니 얼어 잘가 하노라.

Yim Je

This Shijo is given to a kisayng, a geisha, named Harn-woo, meaning 'cold rain', and here's her immediate response.

한우:
어이 얼어 잘이 므스 일 얼어 잘이
원앙침(鴛鴦枕) 비취금(翡翠衾) 어듸 두고 얼어 자리
오늘은 찬 비 맛자신이 녹아 잘까 하노라

Why sleep frozen, for what to sleep frozen,
when there are lovebird pillows and jade bed cover?
Today, soaked in the cold rain, so might as well sleep melt.

< On the owl >

Though the dethroned lord
yearns after his old palace,
sadly, he can't go back there
only to remain in the South.
A piece of mournful weeps
sound like the moment of death.
And then now,
only the moon shines bright
on the branches of sweetbriers.

Kim On Seong

When this baby was born to us,
we brought her up, with her hair braided.
Time has flown so fast that
now she is fully grown up.
The baby is,
now following about after the lord,
with lamp in the hand, in the court.

Kim On Seong

咏子規	자규를 읊다.
帝子思巴國	쫓겨난 임금이 파촉을 그리워해도
江南怨未歸	강남에서 원통하게 돌아가지 못하네.
一聲啼欲斷	한마디 울음소리 숨 끊어질 듯
明月海棠枝	해당화 가지에는 달만 밝구나.

Yim Je

나니 저 아이를
머리 땋아 길렀더니
세월이 덧없어
어이 그리 자라건고
그 아이
옥등에 불 켜들고
님을 좇아 다니거다.

Jarng Hyern

Where is my prince going now,
when sun's set on Aprok river?
How could he be going even to Peking,
which is away thousands of miles?
When the grass,
gets green and green in the spring time,
just come back in no time.

xxxii

Park Jae Woo

Water flows from Fairy's Bridge
to the town of Purple Mist.
Only the sound from the water remains
for the Kingdom Half Millennium.
My little boy,
Whoever would bother to ask after
the ups and downs of this ancient homeland?

xxxiii

Lee Jeong Eun

압록강 해진 후에
어여쁜 우리 님이
연운만리(燕雲萬里)를
어디라고 가시는고
봄풀이
푸르고 푸르거든
즉시 돌아오소서.

Jarng Hyern

선인교(仙人橋) 나린 물이
자하동에 흘러들어
반천년(半千年) 왕업(王業)이
물소리 뿐이로다.
아이야
고국흥망(故國興亡)을
물어 무삼하리오.

Jerng Do-jern (1342 ~ 1398)

Should this body die and die,
even should die for a hundred times
and should the bones turn to dirt,
with or without a piece of soul,
Will it ever,
cease to be, will it ever go away,
the single heart of mine for my lord?

Park Jae Woo

Snowy heron, don't you go to the valley,
where crows are fighting each other.
Angered crows will feel jealous
of your color, clean and white.
I am afraid,
that the well cleaned body of yours,
might be stained by the crows.

Han Jae Eun

이 몸이 죽고 죽어
一百番 고쳐 죽어
白骨이 塵土되여
넋이라도 있고 없고
님 向한
一片丹心이야
가실 줄이 있으랴.

Jerng Mong-joo (1337 ~ 1392)

까마귀 싸우는 골에
백로야 가지 마라
성난 까마귀
흰 빛을 새오나니
淸江에
좋이 씻은 몸을
더럽힐까 하노라.

Mother of Jerng Mong-ju or Kim Jerng goo

Old man there, carrying the baggage,
on the head and on the back,
put the baggage down onto me.
I am young, so will even rocks feel heavy?
How could you,
even carry baggage yourself,
when you are already sad enough to be old.

Park Jae Woo

Flowers bloomed in the night rain
the shool is ripe by this time.
My dear friend with the ker moon go,
promised to visit me along with the bright moon.
Dear kid,
the moon has risen up over the eaves,
so look out who is coming!

Lee Jeong Eun

이고 진 저 늙은이
짐 벗어 나를 주오
나는 젊었거늘
돌인들 무거우랴
늙기도
설워라커늘
짐을조차 지실까.

Jerng Cherl (1536 ~ 1593)

꽃은 밤비에 피고
빚은 술 다 익거다.
거문고 가진 벗이
달 함께 오마터니
아이야
모첨(茅簷)에 달 올랐다
벗님 오나 보아라.

Jerng Cherl

The two Buddha, naked and starved
face each other, on the roadside
rain or wind, snow or frost
they will only have to suffer.
They never know,
human separation,
I do envy the two Buddha.

Lee Kyung-hoon

Wild geese all flown away
leaving behind bites of frost,
autumn nights long and long
sick in nostalgia deep and deep,
Hence I suppose,
shiny moon in the yard
shows me my hometown good and old.

Lee Jeong Eun

길 위에 두 돌부처
벗고 굶고 마주 서서
바람 비 눈서리를
맞도록 맞을 망정
인간에
이별을 모르니
그를 불워 하노라.

Jerng Cherl

기러기 다 날아가고
서리는 몇 번 온고
秋夜도 김도 길샤
客愁도 하도 하다
밤중만
滿庭月色이
고향 본 듯 하여라.

Jo Myerng-ree (1697 ~ 1756)

Hempen dressed in winter days,
exposed to snow rain in the caves,
though never have I received
any patches of clouded sunshine,
but never can I,
stop tears gathering in my eyes
when I hear the sun had sunk to the western hill.

xxxiv

Lee Jeong Eun

It sprinkled down on the pond
and it's foggy at the willow limbs.
The ferryman, where's he gone,
and the boat, why's it tied alone?
A seagull,
probably mate lost, comes and goes,
flying about the glow of the sunset.

Park Jae Woo

삼동에 베옷 입고 암혈에 눈비 맞아
구름 낀 볕뉘도 쬔 적이 없건마는
서산에 해지다 하니 눈물겨워 하노라.

Jo Shik (1501 ~ 1572)

한역가
三冬衣葛棲巖穴 曾未向陽沛雨雪
聞說西山日已昏 不禁涕淚空嗚咽

樂高 849

지당(池塘)에 비 뿌리고
양류(楊柳)에 내 끼인 제
사공(沙工)은 어듸 가고
뷘 배만 매엿난고
석양에
짝 일흔 갈며기는
오락가락 하노매라.

Jo Hern (544 ~ 1592)

To say something is said to be vulgar,
and to say nothing is said to be ignorant.
If poverty is laughed at and
wealth is only coveted by,
in what way,
can I fare well or live well,
under this heaven along with others.

Han Jae Eun

As the night comes to town
a dog barks from afar.
I open the twig gate and I see
the moon against the cold sky.
You dog there,
What would you do by barking there
at the moon asleep o'er the empty mountain?

Park Jae Woo

말 하면 잡류(雜類)라 하고
말 아니면 어리다 하네
빈한(貧寒)을 남이 웃고
부귀(富貴)를 새오는데
아마도
이 하늘 아래서
살올 일이 어려웨라

Joo Ui-shik

산촌(山村)에 밤이 드니
먼뒷 개 즈져온다
시비(柴扉)를 열고 보니
하늘이 챠고 달이로다.
뎌 개야
공산(空山) 잠든 달을
즈져 므삼하리오.

Chern Kum

The white sun falls to the West
and Yellow river flows to the East Sea.
Is it like this that all heroes
will fall down in the Mt. Book marng?
Let it be,
as the living are bound to ups and downs,
would there be anything to sigh about?

Lee Jeong Eun

Do not draw out a straw cushion,
this leaf cushion's grateful enough.
Do not kindle the pine oil lamp,
last night's moon is rising up.
Little boy,
cheapest drink stuffs will do,
just bring out all, don't spare any.

Park Jae Woo

白日은 西山에 지고
黃河는 東海로 든다.
古來 영웅이
북망(北邙)으로 드단 말가.
두어라
물유성쇠(物有盛衰)니
한(恨)할 줄이 있으랴'

Choy Choong (984 ~ 1068)

짚 방석 내지 마라
낙엽엔들 못 앉으랴
솔불 혀지 마라
어제 진 달 돋아 온다
아희야
박주 산챌망정
없다 말고 내어라

xxxv

Harn Ho (1543 ~ 1605)

Mountains are highly high
and waters are longly long.
Amid high mountains and long waters,
nowhere have I to go to.
My sleeves,
soaked from missing you, my dear lord,
when should it dry, never do I know.

Park Jae Woo

< Grieving May charng's death >
Beautiful words were like silk spread
and crystal clear songs stopped running clouds.
Eating the stolen peach in the heaven,
she had to come down to this earth.
How could she leave the earth?
I wonder if she was punished for stealing the elixir of life.
In lotus bunting, light is dim,
and on the jade skirt, the scent still lingers.
The coming years, when peach blossoms abloom,
who'd come visit the grave of Serl do .

xxxvi

Han Jae Eun

뫼는 높으나 높고
물은 기나 길다.
높은 뫼 긴 물에
갈 길도 그지 없다.
님 그려
젖은 소매는
어느 적에 마를꼬.

Her Garng (1520 ~ 1592)

< 매창의 죽음을 슬퍼하며 >
아름다운 글귀는 비단 펼쳐놓은 듯
맑은 노래, 구름도 멈추게 했네.
복숭아 훔쳐 먹고 이 세상에 내려와서
불사약 훔쳤던가 이승을 떠나다니.
부용꽃 휘장에 등불은 희미한데
비취색 치마엔 향기 아직 남았네.
명년에 복사꽃 필 때쯤이면
설도의 무덤을 그 누가 찾을는지.

Her Gyoon (1569 ~ 1618)

All the mountains and the vast nature
I will see them from my seat.
When the lifeless rivers also
flow around in respect for the Lord,
A man of strategy,
will he ever let worn away
the noble ambitions and great policies of his in his pocket?

Kim On Seong

I picked out a branch of wild willow
to have it sent to you.
I do hope that you plant it
by the window of your bedroom.
If you see,
a new sprout the next day,
it's me that budded out by the night drizzle.

Lee Jeong Eun

호산(湖山) 천만리(千萬里)를
앉아서 다 보과라.
무정한 강한(江漢)도
조종우해(朝宗于海) 하거든
하물며
대장부 제세장책(濟世長策)을
품 안에서 늙히랴.

Her Jar (1496~1551)

묏버들 갈해 것거
보내노라 님의 손대.
자시난 창 밧긔
심거 두고 보쇼셔.
밤비예
새닙곳 나거든
날인가도 너기쇼셔.

Hong Rarng

You Blue Stream in this Green Mountain,
do not boast your fast ride.
To come back may be so hard,
once you reach the big ocean.
Then how about,
making a good night of today
when the moonshine fills the mountain?

Lee Kyung-hoon

The old mountain's all the same,
but the old water's far from the same.
Day and night, flowing down on
can it ever not be changed?
The big heroes,
aren't they like the flowing water?
once gone then, they never return.

Lee Kyung-hoon

청산리(靑山裏) 벽계수(碧溪水) ㅣ야
수이 감을 자랑마라
일도창해(一到滄海)하면
다시 오기가 어려오니
명월이 만공산(滿空山)하니
쉬여간들 엇더리.

Hwarng Jin-yi

[漢譯歌] 碧溪水 ;
靑山影裡碧溪水 容易東流爾莫誇
一到滄海難再見 且留明月暎娑婆

<申緯 : 小樂府>

산은 옛 산이로되
물은 옛 물이 아니로다.
주야(晝夜)에 흐르거든
옛 물이 있을손가.
인걸(人傑)도
물과 같도다.
가고 아니 오는 것은

Hwarng Jin-yi

Oh, my, did I not know,
that I will miss him again?
Had I only asked him to stay,
would he have left me so?
I never know,
why did I have him leave
and why do I miss him so.

xxxvii

Lee Jeong Eun

Have I ever been unfaithful?
Had I ever deceived you?
Yet you seem never to come
to me in this deepest night.
Whenever the leaves,
scatter about in the autumn wind
my heart always pounds by that sound.

Lee Jeong Eun

어져 내 일이야 그릴 줄을 모로다냐
이시라 하더면 가랴마는 제 구태야
보내고 그리는 情은 나도 몰라 하노라.

Hwarng Jin-yi

내 언제 무신(無信)하여 님을 언제 속였관데
월침 삼경(月沈三更)에 올 뜻이 전혀 없네.
추풍(秋風)에 지는 잎 소리야 낸들 어이 하리오.

Hwarng Jin-yi

*** 한역가: <李民宬 : 敬亭集>

我來豈無信　月沉夜三更　秋風自落葉　非我惱君情

響屧疑 ; <申緯 : 小樂府>
寡信何曾瞞著麽　　月沈無意夜經過
颯然響地吾何與　　原是秋風落葉多

I'll cut out some big chunks
off the long, long winter night
to keep them roll by roll
deep in the closet, in the Spring Yibool
Then, I will
spread it bend by bend
the short night when he comes.

xxxviii

Lee Kyung-hoon

In the dream of last night
received a letter from my love
I read it a hundred times
And placed it on my chest
The very letter's
not especially heavy but
it feels so on the chest.

Lee Kyung-hoon

동지달 기나긴 밤을
한 허리를 버혀 내여
춘풍 이불 아래
서리허리 넣었다가
어론 님
오신 날 밤이여든
구비구비 펴리라

Hwarng Jin-yi

[漢譯歌] 冬至永夜 ;
截取冬之夜半强　　春風被裡屈蟠藏
燈明酒爛郎來夕　　曲曲鋪成折折長　　(申緯:小樂府)

간 밤에 꿈을 꾸니
님에게서 편지 왔네
일백번 다시 보고
가슴 위에 얹어두니
각별히
무겁진 아니해도
가슴 답답하여라.

Wild geese now all flown away,
who will carry my long message?
So, I tried to have a dream,
only to fail, sleep never came.
Even my dreams,
must have been taken away
by the Neem, my naughty Neem.

Lee Kyung-hoon

I surely wish that my tears
were the pearls that I could
save them up to seat him
among the pearls when he returns.
But the tears,
just go away with no trace,
as soon as they are down.

Lee Kyung-hoon

기러기 다 날아가니
소식을 뉘 전하리
꿈이나 꾸자 하니
잠이 와야 꿈 아니 꾸랴
꿈조차
가져간 님을
생각하여 무엇하리.

눈물이 진주라면
흐르지 않게 싸두었다가
십 년 후 오신 임을
구슬성에 앉히련만
흔적이
이내 없으니
그를 설워하노라.

As my horse suddenly startles
I look down grabbing the harness tight.
What a mountain gorgeous and green,
is submerged under the river!
My dear horse,
don't you be scared ‘cause
I just meant to take a good look.

Kim On Seong

How can I stop by myself
the spring already resolved to be gone?
How could it just disappear
with peach and plum still in the bud?
My little one,
filter me over the half matured shool,
‘cause I have to go see off the spring.

Kim On Seong

말(馬)이 놀나거늘
혁(革) 잡고 굽어 보니
금수청산(錦繡靑山)이
물 속에 잠겨세라.
뎌 말아
놀나지 마라
이을 보려 하노라.

봄이 가려 하니
내라 혼자 말릴 쏜가
다 못 핀 도리화를
어찌하고 가려는다.
아이야
덜 괸 술 걸러라
가는 봄 전송하리라.

Home brewed shool finally ran out,
then a pal came from afar.
Though a pub is near here
what can be offered for this old clothes?
My little child,
don't try to make up a fake deal
just bring us what little they offer.

Kim On Seong

Love gathers to be fire,
and it blooms in the heart,
liver gets rotten to be water,
and seeps out through the eyes.
Water and fire,
attacking me simultaneously,
who could be well in this bodily state?

Han Jae Eun

빚은 술 다 먹으니
먼데서 벗이 왔다
술집은 제연마는
헌옷에 언마 주리.
아희야
셔기지 말고
주는 대로 받아라.

사랑 모여 불이 되여
가슴에 피어나고
간장(肝腸) 썩어 물이 되여
두 눈으로 솟아난다
一身이
水火 상침(相侵) 하니
살동말동 하여라

Does everybody happen to have a lover?
Is every break up sad for all?
This is the love, first in my life,
and the best that I could get.
Should we meet,
some day again, I will take it,
our true destiny, me and him.

Han Jae Eun

Do not blow, mischievous wind
when the window's full of snowy moon.
I surely knew that it was not
the sound coming from his feet.
Nevertheless,
I cannot but wonder if it is,
whenever I miss him and long for him.

Lee Jeong Eun

사랑인들 님마다 하며
이별인들 다 셜우랴
평생에 처음이오
다시 못 어더볼 님이로다
이후에
다시 만나면
연분인가 하노라.

설월(雪月)이 만창(滿窓)한듸
바람아 부지 마라
예리성(曳履聲) 아닌 줄을
판연(判然)히 알건마난
그립고
아쉬온 적이면
행혀 귄가하노라.

Part 2: Modern Shijo

< Sunset glow >

Look
at the fate
fading out spitting blood.

The solemn adieu,
rather beautiful,
even enchanting
when yearnings boil and overflow
like wild rage.

How could I
bear such pain!
How could I
bear such love!

At sunset
the sea falls into the shadow of blossoms
along the crimson wave.

xxxix

Lee Jeong Eun

< 노을 >

저
피 토하며 꺼져 가는
운명을 보라.
애절함이 분노처럼 끓어 넘치는
차라리 황홀하고도
아름다운
장엄한 이별

저토록
처절한 아픔을 어이하리
저토록
처절한 사랑을 어이하리
해질 녘
붉은 물결에
꽃 그늘로 지는 바다.

Ban Yung ho

< The mountain says that it stands still
not being able to cross the river >

And the river says,
that it runs around since
it cannot cross the mountain.

Han Jae Eun

< Reed >

Like a flower,
you blossomed a flower
which isn't a flower shaped like a flower.

Park Jae Woo

< Would regret whether I do it or not do it >

That flower there,
Shall I pick it up or
shall I just leave it there?

Lee Kyung-hoon

< 저 산은 너를 건너지
못해 서 있다 하고 >

강물은
널 넘지 못해
돌아간다 하네.

Ban Yung ho

< 갈대 >

꽃인 듯
꽃도 아닌 꽃을
꽃처럼 피웠구나

Ban Yung ho

< 꺾으면 후회하고 꺾잖아도 후회할 >

저 꽃을
꺾어갈거나
그냥 보고 갈거나

Ban Yung ho

< Sunset glow >

Even a ritual
shutting down the sky,
would it be ever so magnificent?

Lee Kyung-hoon

< Snail >

A journey,
a far away journey of penance
that goes through by reading Braille.

Han Jae Eun

< Love is >

A joy,
it must be and also,
a sadness in other words.

Lee Jeong Eun

< 노을 >
하늘을
닫는 의식이
저토록 장엄할까

Ban Yung ho

< 달팽이 >
점자를
읽으며 가는
멀고도 먼 고행길

Ban Yung ho

< 사랑이란 >
그것은
기쁨이려니
달리는 슬픔이야

Ban Yung ho

< Time and tide >
Dear fellow there,
Is it you that is going,
Or is it me that is going ahead?

Lee Kyung-hoon

< Poets >
Would complete
what he says while
he restrains his words.

Han Jae Eun

< Wife >
Rising,
as a dim day moon
as if there is, as if there isn't.

Han Jae Eun

< 세월 >
인석아
네가 가느냐
아님, 내가 가는 거냐

Ban Yung ho

< 시인은 >
할 말을
자제하면서
제 할 말을 다하지

Ban Yung ho

< 아내 >
희미한
낮달로 떠서
있는 듯 없는 듯이

Ban Yung ho

< From mind to mind >
Lake Blue,
is blue from the mind
that is filled with the sky.

Park Jae Woo

< Human nature >
The butterfly
hanging around at the garden
left at once as the flowers fell.

Lee Kyung-hoon

< Bell in the temple >
A carp
gets enlightened
while the Buddha is fast asleep.

Han Jae Eun

< 이심전심 >

호수가
푸르른 것은
하늘빛을 담은 맘

Ban Yung ho

< 인지상정 >

꽃밭에
노닐던 나비
꽃이 지니 떠났네

Ban Yung ho

< 풍경 소리 >

부처가
잠든 사이에
붕어가 깨우치네.

Ban Yung ho

< The leper >
The leper was ashamed at the brightness
of the sun and the sky.
When the moon rose up
in the field of barley,
he ate a baby
and he wept a weep,
ruddy as flower, all night long.

xl

Park Jae Woo

Don't you praise the Mt. Kum karng,
only maple leaves now turned red.
The maple trees leaf by leaf
only boast their gorgeous color.
I'd rather be,
welcoming the cutting wind
in the great Mongolian desert.

Lee Kyung-hoon

< 문둥이 >
해와 하늘 빛이
문둥이는 서러워
보리밭에 달 뜨면
애기 하나 먹고
꽃처럼 붉은 우름을
밤새 우렀다.

So Chong Ju (1915 ~ 2000)

금강산 좋다 마라
단풍만 피었더라
단풍의 잎새 잎새
秋色만 자랑터라
차라리
몽고 대사막에
大風을 반기리라.

Shin Chay ho (1880 ~ 1936)

< Missing him >

You stay away from the thought,
you'll forget him, that's what they say.
Amid the living, hectic and harsh,
when I assumed it's all forgotten....
On the way,
the longing suddenly crowds
in my heart and fill it up.

Lee Kyung-hoon

< Sweet home >

Kid reads a book
I do embroidery.
Lampwick turned up
and brow to brow.
Even darkness,
surrounds us as if
in reverence for the affection around.

Lee Jeong Eun

< 그리움 >

생각을 멀리하면
잊을 수도 있다는데
고된 살음에
잊었는가 하다가도
가다가
월컥 한 가슴
밀고 드는 그리움.

Yi Young do (1916 ~ 1976)

< 團欒 (단란) >

아이는 글을 읽고
나는 繡(수)를 놓고
심지 돋우고
이마를 맞대이면
어둠도
고운 愛情에
삼간한 듯 둘렸다.

Yi Young do (1916 ~ 1976)

< No title 1 >

If he comes, I get embarrassed
if he doesn't, I feel sad.
Listening out for his voice,
that might be already around.
I would hope,
for his visit to me,
day by day and all day long.

When we have seats face to face,
all my words are swallowed in.
Two of us with weary hearts
would only look out the window.
Then he would
rise up from the seat and go.
I see him leave only looking on.

Park Jae Woo

< 무제　1 >

오면 민망하고
아니오면 서글프고
행여나 그 음성
귀 기울여 기다리며
때로는 종일을 두고
바라기도 하니라.

정작 마주 앉으면
말은 도로 없어지고
서로 야윈 가슴
먼 창만 바라다가
그대로 일어서 가면
하염없이 보내니라.

Yi Young do

< Early spring haze >

When your breath touches me,
as if fondling on the cheek,
my love then is azirang'ee,
arjirarng'yi of early spring.
In the field
yellow with radish stalks

Butterfly
                    Butterfly
Butterfly
                    Butterfly

xli

Park Jae Woo

< 아지랑이 >

어루만지듯
당신
숨결
이마에 다사하면
내 사랑은 아지랑이
춘삼월 아지랑이
장다리
노오란 텃밭에

나비
　　　　　　　　　　나비
나비
　　　　　　　　　　나비

Yi Young do

< A gingko Tree >

Flowerless through
the years of long youth.
Standing only to look on,
inwardly boiling the hot blood.
Decoration,
being rather extravagant for him,
he throws down those golden clothes.

Park Jae Woo

< Precipice >

Am I not equal to open?
Is the door not to be opened?
Your breath I surely feel
on the vessels of my blood.
Is it that,
you already turned about on me,
ever the more as I knock and shake?

Park Jae Woo

< 은행나무 >
꽃 한 송이 피우지 못한 채
기나 긴 청춘의 날을
멀거니 바라만 섰기로
안으로 끓이던 그 피
차라리
치장도 겨웁네
훨 훨 벗는 황금의상

Yi Young do

< 절벽 >
못 여는 것입니까?
안 열리는 문입니까?
당신 숨결은
내 핏줄에 느끼는데
흔들고
두드려도 한결
돌아앉은 뜻입니까?

Yi Young do

< Pagoda 3 >

You are already away that far,
I stand here still yet, and.....
The heaven and earth I turned about in,
even without a gesture of waving hand.
My longings,
let it gather into the sariras
and then harden into a blue rock.

Lee Jeong Eun

< Footprints >

I hated spring, it's too gorgeous
I hated autumn, too transparent.
On a night, snow piles up
like a memory and light is afar.
You stamp steps,
and I keep walking by,
just keep walking by after your steps.

Lee Kyung-hoon

< 塔 3 >

너는 저만치 가고
나는 여기 섰는데.....
손 한번 흔들지 못한 채
돌아선 하늘과 땅
愛慕는
舍利로 맺혀
푸른 돌로 굳어라.

Yi Young do

< 발자국 >

봄은 화려해 미웠고
가을은 투명해 싫었다.
추억처럼 눈이 쌓이고
불빛 머나 먼 밤을
한 자욱
한 자욱 네가 고이며
나는 걷기만 하네.

Yi Ho woo (1912 ~ 1970)

< Crack >

I had had to learn despair
and here and now, I meet this rock.
Rain falls and wind blows
upon its countless wrinkles and seams.
Time and tide,
must be hurting this solid rock.
Look, another fissure now forms.

Park Jae Woo

< 금 >

차라리 절망을 배워
바위 앞에 섰습니다.
무수한 주름살 위에
비가 오고 바람이 붑니다.
바위도
세월이 아픈가
또 하나 금이 갑니다.

Yi Ho woo

< Before you >

What is it that brought me here?
Unable to sleep in long nights,
who once was living out merrily
amid laughter loud and easy.
I may rather,
throw my life before you,
to perish away and to sink.

I loved you so, so I could not say so,
love is now piling up high
however hard I sweep it out.
This day too,
I may as well go on,
just thinking about you, remembering you.

Park Jae Woo

< 너 앞에 >

한바탕 웃음으로
쉽게 살아온 내
어이다가 이리도
잠 못는 몸 되었을꼬
이 목숨
차라리 너 앞에
던져 버리고 지라.

하 이리 너를 아끼어
말 한번 차마 못한 채
쓸고 쓸어도
정은 쌓여만 가오
이 날도
너를 생각는만으로
보람하여 살꺼나.

Yi Ho woo

< Living along I >

Flowers are bloomed only
as they are supposed to.
No one ever told them to
nor they wanted even a glance.
Any reason,
was it ever required for?
You and me living this very day.

Lee Jeong Eun

< Illusion >
Everyone goes and goes
You and I go and go.
Something over there
comes and comes here.
The heaven,
as always is only laughing like that
with mouth open, so wide open.

Lee Jeong Eun

< 영위 I >

피기로 마련이었기
꽃들은 피어 있을 뿐
뉘 피래서 핌이 아닐레
뉘 보라 핌은 더욱 아닐레
너나 내 이 날에 사는 일
무얼 따져 하리야.

Yi Ho woo

< 환 >

모두들 가고만 있는데
너도 나도 가고만 있는데
무엇인가 무엇인가
자꾸만 오는 것 있다
하늘은 노상 저렇게
허벌레 웃고만 있고

Yi Ho woo

< A piece of remembrance >
It was a freezing night
I had coffee over and over
without words you only snapped
a bunch of matchsticks.
That moment hence,
you and I walked along
different paths and different lives.

Lee Jeong Eun

< Pomegranate >
How crude my face is?
How rough my lips are?
How dare I try to tell you
all the meaning of redness berry by berry
Take a look,
hey take a look over here,
the broken and uncovered chest of mine.

Han Jae Eun

< 회상 >
몹시 추운 밤이었다
나는 커피만 거듭하고
너는 말없이 자꾸
성냥개비를 꺾기만 했다.
그것이 서로의 인생의
갈림길이었구나.

Yi Ho woo

< 석류 >
투박한 나의 얼굴
두툴한 나의 입술
알알이 붉은 뜻을
내가 어이 이르리까
보소라 임아 보소라
빠개 젖힌
이 가슴.

Jo Woon (1900 ~ ?)

< A Violet >

There's one small flower
that vaguely says hello to me.
A violet, abloom lonely
at the rock pile of the roadside.
Did you not,
didn't you also look at me
just as I looked at you?

Han Jae Eun

< 오랑캐꽃 >

넌지시 알은 체 하는
한 작은 꽃이 있다.
길가 돌담불에
외로이 핀 오랑캐꽃
너 또한 나를 보기를
나
너 보듯 했더냐.

Jo Woon

Part 3: Other verses

Here are some verses that are Coreans' favorites. Even if these are not Shijo, the verses here could be said to express the core of the Corean heart.

You live with no words!
The green mountain shows me,
You live with no flaws!
The bright moon shines me.
Greed put down, anger taken off,
like winds and like clouds,
they tell me to live so.

Han Jae Eun

청산은 나를 보고
말없이 살라 하고
명월은 나를 보고
티없이 살라 하네
욕심도 벗어놓고
성냄도 벗어놓고
바람같이 구름같이
살다가 가라 하네.

Zen Master Nar ong (1320 ~ 1376)

< Pleasure and agony >

A walker under heavy load
don’t be looking only your steps.
Sometimes look up at the view
around the world which is cool.

Sweet or sour's in the mouth
success or failure's in the mind.
After sunset rises the moon
Rest a while in the nasty nights.

A walker under heavy load
don’t complain on the steep path.
Sometimes give a break to yourself,
give a thought to the highway coming.

Comfort can be a seed of pain,
pain can be a seed of pleasure.
Look, you could grow golden corns
in a land barren as desert.

< 고락 >

무거운 짐 지고서 닫는 사람은
기구한 발뿌리만 보지 말고서
때로는 고개들어 사방 산천의
시원한 세상 풍경 바라 보시오.

먹이의 달고 씀은 입에 달리고
영욕의 苦와 樂도 맘에 달렸소
보시오 해가져도 달이 뜬다오
그믐밤 날 궂거든 쉬어 가시오.

무거운 짐 지고서 닫는 사람은
숨차다 고갯길을 탄치 말고서
때로는 맘을 눅여 탄탄대로의
이제도 있을 것을 생각하시오.

편안이 괴로움의 씨도 되고요
쓰림은 즐거움의 씨도 됩니다
보시오 火田망정 갈고 심으면
가을에 황금이삭 수북 달리오.

A girl threw herself in the water,
her life being a dance on the blade
Maybe she is right and correct,
but she didn't know the other way.

Her life being dancing on the blade,
but she did dance on her own.
Who told her to dance the dance?
How crooked must she've been.

She had really asked for that
and she is now blaming other people.
A walker under heavy load,
rest a while at a roadside field.

A walker under heavy load,
don't be looking only your steps.
Sometimes look up to the world,
changing along the four of seasons.

칼날위에 춤추는 인생이라고
물속에 몸을 던진 몹쓸 계집애
어쩌면 그럴듯도 하긴 하지만
그렇지 않은 줄은 왜 몰랐던고.

칼날 위에 춤추는 인생이라고
자기가 칼날 위에 춤을 춘 게지
그 누가 미친 춤을 추라 했나요
얼마나 비꼬이운 계집애든가.

야말로 제 고생을 제가 사서는
잡을 데 다시없어 엄나무지요
무거운 짐 지고서 닫는 사람은
길가의 청풀밭에 쉬어 가시오.

무거운 짐 지고서 닫는 사람은
기구한 발뿌리만 보지 말고서
때로는 춘하추동 사방산천의
뒤바뀌는 세상도 바라 보시오.

Can you get your load off?
Can you give your way up?
A walker under heavy load,
Look at a water drop on the stream.

Drops of water if gathered,
will flow down to be ocean waves
will go up to be clouds,
and will come down to be the rains

If rained water gather and gather
it's waterfalls into hydropower,
it's irrigation into fertile field,
it's oil for dry burning land.

It is to be a nice cool dew
for the withered, thirsty pretty flowers.
It is to be a nice cool fountain
for a walker thirsty and lonely.

무겁다 이 짐을랑 벗을 겐가요
괴롭다 이 길을랑 아니 걷겠나
무거운 짐 지고서 닫는 사람은
보시오 시내 위의 물 한방울을.

한방울 물이라도 모둥켜지면
흘러가서 바다의 물결됩니다
하늘로 올라가서 구름됩니다
다시금 땅에 내려 비가 됩니다.

비되어 내린 물이 모둥켜지면
산간엔 폭포되어 수력전기요
들에선 관개되어 만종석이요
메말라 타는 땅엔 기름입니다.

어여쁜 꽃 한가지 이울어 갈 제
밤에 찬이슬 되어 추겨도 주고
외로운 어느 길손 창자조릴 제
길가의 찬샘 되어 늦꿔도 주오.

Even every drop of water
has the meaning of its running.
Who could ever blame this path?
Who that is so self-centered?

Heavy load has its meaning,
painful load has its meaning.
A walker under heavy load,
is truly humane in this world.

Park Jae Woo

시내의 여지 없는 물한방울도
흐르는 그만 뜻이 이러하거든
어느 인생 하나이 저만 저라고
기구하다 이 길을 타발 나요

이 짐이 무거움에 뜻이 있고요
이 짐이 괴로움에 뜻이 있다오
무거운 짐 지고서 닫는 사람이
이 세상 사람다운 사람이라오.

Kim So werl (1902 ~ 1934)

< Unforgettable >

It would linger around.
Hope you pass on through somehow.
Time and tide might drown the memory.

It would linger around.
Hope you bide the time somehow.
Time and tide might fade it a little.

But still one end would be like this;
Unforgettable it sure is,
How could I keep the thought away?

Lee Jeong Eun

< 못 잊어 >

못 잊어 생각이 나겠지요
그런대로 한 세상 지내시구려
사노라면 잊힐 날 있으리다

못 잊어 생각이 나겠지요
그런대로 세월만 가라시구려
못 잊어도 더러는 잊히오리다

그러나 또 한끝 이렇지요
그리워 살틀히 못 잊는데
어쩌면 생각이 떠지나요?

Kim So werl

< Azalea >

If you leave tired of me,
I'll let go without any words.
Yerng byern, Yark sarn azaleas
shall be scattered along your way.
Do gently ever stamp on
the blossoms laid, step by step.
If you leave sick of me,
never shall I shed a single tear.

Lee Jeong Eun

< 진달래꽃 >

나 보기가 역겨워 가실 때에는
말없이 고히 보내 드리우리다
寧邊에 藥山 진달래꽃
아름 따다 가실 길에 뿌리 우리다
가시는 걸음걸음 놓인 그 꽃을
사뿐히 즈려밟고 가시 옵소서
나 보기가 역겨워 가실 때에는
죽어도 아니 눈물 흘리우리다.

Kim So werl

< Round Sun >

Round sun's coming up
Round sun's giggling
Being itself without cease
Round sun's caught on fire.

Whenever it rises up,
My heart leaps with joy.
To your sound of laugh,
My heart pounds with joy.

Be the water, you round sun
Round sun's your laugh.
Be the fire, you round sun
Round sun's your heart.

He was hiding himself
In the mysterious night light.
You laugh laughter
In the love, love itself.

< 둥근 해>

솟아온다 둥근 해
해족인다 둥근 해
끊임없이 그 자체
타고 있는 둥근 해

그가 솟아올 때면
내 가슴이 뛰논다
너의 웃음소리에
내 가슴이 뛰논다

물이 되랴 둥근 해
둥근 해는 네 웃음
불이 되랴 둥근 해
둥근 해는 네 마음

그는 숨어 있었다
신비로운 밤빛에
너의 웃는 웃음은
사랑이란 그 안에

He walks every day
On the sky end less.
Your heart swims about
In the ocean called 'the life'.

Under your bright shine
Green grasses spring up.
Before your laughter,
My hair grows up.

Round sun burning on
Is the laughter of my love.
Open gate at Sky East
Is the face of my love.

Han Jae Eun

그는 매일 걷는다.
끝이 없는 하늘을
너의 맘은 헴친다
생명이란 바다를

밝은 그 별 아래선
푸른 풀이 자란다
너의 웃음 앞에선
내 머리가 자란다

불이 붙는 둥근 해
내 사랑의 웃음은
동편 하늘 열린 문
내 사랑의 얼굴은

Kim So werl

< Somewhere after some time >

I do not recall the name
But the eye and lip
Is carved in my heart.

When it rains, or winds
I cannot help but remember
The night in the shadow by the lamp

Love leaves
Past remains
Lakeside in the summer
The park in the autumn

On the bench
The leaves fall
The leaves turn to dirt
And even if our love fades away
Covered under the leaves

I do not recall the name
But the eye and lip
Is carved in my heart
In the heart, my cool heart.

Lee Jeong Eun

< 세월이 가면 >

지금 그 사람의 이름은 잊었지만
그의 눈동자 입술은
내 가슴에 있어

바람이 불고
비가 올 때도
나는 저 유리창 밖
가로등 그늘의 밤을 잊지 못하네

사랑은 가고
과거는 남는 것
여름날의 호숫가
가을의 공원

그 벤치 위에
나뭇잎은 떨어지고
나뭇잎은 흙이 되고
나뭇잎에 덮여서
우리들 사랑이 사라진다 해도

지금 그 사람의 이름은 잊었지만
그의 눈동자 입술은
내 가슴에 있어
내 서늘한 가슴에 있건만.

Park In hwarn (1926 ~ 1956)

< Beside the Chrysanthemum >

To blossom one flower of Chrysanthemum,
a cuckoo might've been chirping so, since spring time.

To blossom one flower of Chrysanthemum,
thunder might have been roaring so, in dark clouds.

Flower, you look like my sister,
who is come back from the far-away youth,
when her mind had been arrested by yearnings and regrets,
who now stands in front of the mirror.

To blossom your yellow petals,
the frost had fallen so last night,
and no slumber would come to me.

Park Jae Woo

< 국화 옆에서 >

한송이의 국화꽃을 피우기 위해
봄부터 소쩍새는
그렇게 울었나 보다

한송이의 국화꽃을 피우기 위해
천둥은 먹구름 속에서
또 그렇게 울었나 보다

그립고 아쉬움에 가슴 조이던
머언 먼 젊음의 뒤안길에서
인제는 돌아와 거울 앞에 선
내 누님같이 생긴 꽃이여

노오란 네 꽃잎이 피려고
간밤엔 무서리가 저리 내리고
내게는 잠도 오지 않았나 보다.

So Chong Ju (1915 ~ 2000)

Part 4: Epilogues

After I finished the Shijo translation

Han Jae Eun

Naughty classical literature. The words were like a difficult math problem. I remember my first impression of "Koowoon-mong (Title: A nine-layer dream, a major Corean old novel)", an assignment to be finished before the date of entrance to High School. I still vividly remember, reading the book, I had some tough time with the 17th century language used by hard-to-understand characters, constantly changing terms of reference for people and long-winded literary style.

The beginning of the Shijo translation was almost the same. The prevailing sense of foreignness that I felt when I first tried to translate Shijo cannot be summarized in a few words. Although I didn't know exactly what the verses were trying to say, some vague curiosity started to build in me about Shijo. Then I began to study one by one and step by step, slowly and carefully. In the beginning, it felt too difficult and too demanding. But as I kept on, I started to gain strength. Naturally, I began to have an interest in Classical literature. What had felt so far away from me now came close to me. It turned from a language too difficult to understand into something very meaningful to me. Among other Classical Literature genres, especially to Shijo, I saw my affection grow, the feeling that 'this is mine'. The relationship between me and

Classical Literature turned from nothing to something so close.

Actually, as I came to like Classical Literature, I went on a 'Classcial Literature trip'. When our family was going to travel the South-Western part, famous for its places related with Classical poets, I suggested that Classical Literature should be the theme of our trip. If I hadn't had the chance to translate Shijo, the trip would have been just a plain visit to some famous places with beautiful sceneries. I was never interested in traveling, yet I actively took part in the travel, since the Classical Literature became so meaningful to me through Shijo translation. Before, I was not much interested in traveling and when I went, I just followed my parents' idea. But this time, it was all fun, preparing for the trip and everything and I was really active. The Classical Literature trip was so fulfilling that I could feel first hand the flavor of Classical Literature.

As a student preparing for KSAT where at least one piece of Classical Literature is included, this project was so helpful. In the past, I had to read the Classical Literature presented in the exam in a hurry, but now I am at leisure in reading and solving the problems. Studying old Shijo written by classical writers not only helped me out with reading literature, I became better versed in their view of the world and in their inner world, thus, it led to a better understanding of their works.

Unlike globally well-known Japanese 'Haiku', our Shijo is at a crisis. I was also one of them who contributed to that crisis by not having an interest in Shijo. Now I am on the other side of the line. By translating Shijo, I've become interested in Shijo and I also want to be one of those who can contribute to the preservation and popularization of our beautiful Shijo.

In the process of the translation, there were times when I would ask English speaking foreign people in Corea what they think about my translation. Through our English-translated Shijo, a mutual understanding was possible. It was really marvelous that I was able to convey the way I felt to people who use another language. I could feel how precious a language is. So, I happened to have a keener interest in learning foreign languages.

I want to do a lot for the advancement of Corean Literature to the world through more works with Mr. Lee in the future.

Reflections

Kim On Seong

Recently, I received a pre-publication copy. As this was my first time participating in publishing a book, I was so proud and happy. But also, I felt that I should have devoted more time and that I could have done better. Nevertheless, as a student deeply interested in studying English, it has been good luck for me to take part in this project, and I feel it is very meaningful to have come through this unusual experience along with my school friends.

This book is being published to help foreigners become familiar with Corean Poetry called Shijo. There have been attempts, of course, to translate Shijo into English. But those attempts have been focused mainly on the conveyance of meaning, while this book intends to make the translated pieces fit into the Corean standard Shijo form, so this is not a small difference.

Shijo consists of three Lines, and the first segment of the last Line must be, in Corean Shijo, in 3 syllables. When the structural beauty of a fixed form is combined with good content, there is born a good Shijo, with its unique and indigenous taste. It was for this reason that I found translating Shijo to be so demanding. I had to consider simplicity, the Shijo structure and, as it is a verse, a wise choice of words. Proper nouns in Hangeul were hard to express in English because in English translation, the nouns get too long. These difficulties may have been true for all of us, although the others seemed to overcome them brilliantly. Actually, the most impressive thing about this project was to read other participants' translations. Their translations were simple, they met the complicated requirements, and included neat expressions as well.

The translated works depended solely on our interpretation and translations, as has been intended. Mr. Lee corrected some errors in grammar or vocabulary, but remained silent on everything else to let us think over and revise the Shijo by ourselves. Therefore we had to revise the translations with our utmost efforts. I dare say that these translated Shijo are those that went through our own ceaseless correction process.

We, the new generation are apt to prefer new things to old ones. I, being one of them, have been quite uninterested in spreading, preserving, and developing this precious invaluable Corean culture.

Working on this project, though difficult at many times, I was happy to be reminded of the beauty of Shijo, be it only a little portion of the beauty that I could catch. I felt pride that I am the descendant of our ancestors. It has also greatly inspired me: I am determined to major in English literature.

From the beginning, lots of effort and hearty concern have been given to our project's completion. We had to request permission to use modern Shijo. We had to think about how we would Romanize Corean scripts properly so they could be pronounced as closely as Coreans do. We also asked for the opinions of our friends and family to see what native speakers would think about our verses. Mr. Lee encouraged us to be familiar with related episodes and the poet's life for an extensive understanding of how the poet felt and what their situations were.

There are so many family and friends to thank. First, it is with deepest respect and gratitude that I would like to thank Mr. Lee. His devotion and consistent zeal for the project was most valuable.

I also want to thank our parents and friends who were a constant source of support and encouragement. My laptop-dictionary must also be credited with helping me overcome my poor English composition. Lastly, I hope so dearly that foreigners all over the world come to appreciate the beauty of Shijo and its unique traits, in the same way as Coreans do.

Translating Shijo into English

Lee Jeong Eun

At the very first moment when I decided to join the translation team, I was thinking of the Nobel Prize. People were saying that Corean poets were quite accomplished for sure, however, they would not win the Nobel Prize since there was no translator capable of translating the delicate nuances of Corean into another language. I wasn't content with the fact that the level of literature should be judged by the quality of a translated version, not by the original one. But I realized soon that it is unrealistic to expect an international literary circle to understand Corean language, and that what is most important is to translate the poetry well.

It took almost 2 years to finish the whole work and now I can say that it was worth that much. But in the beginning, this was not the case for a 15-year-old girl who had never read a single line of Shijo. I was pretty much excited at first that I would be the one who introduces Korean literature through English. The higher the expectation, the greater the disappointment, though. I was a little bit worried about English, but not about Corean. Little did I dream that I would be "deciphering" old Corean.

I am used to reading old Corean now, but I was frustrated at that moment. It was more than a hassle to be forced to do some googling to understand my own native tongue. Every time I did not get the grasp of a Shijo, I was dying to quit as I was a girl with no tenacity. I couldn't, though. I was the one who volunteered for it, which means I had to stick to it no matter how stressful it was. I struggled on half-willingly, grumbling at a series of difficulties. After those initial tough days, I began to gain momentum little by little.

When I sent Mr. Lee my rough drafts, he would give me some comments. I remember the first 10 Shijo that I sent to him. They were literally awful, I guess. His comments were like, "Too long to be a poem", "Too arbitrary", "What a cliché", and so on. All the comments that made me grumble have enriched my Shijo and I got to realize that what I had to do was not to translate Corean into English, but to rewrite the poem catering to English speaking people while taking care of its original meaning.

At the same time, I've come to have a different appreciation for the English language. Before I used to compare and contrast Corean, my mother tongue, with English. However, as time passes, I've been able to feel some of the linguistic traits of English. As this is a poetry genre, I dared to omit some prepositions and to change sentence structures, which I had not dared before. I also tried to come up with better expressions than those by the native speakers who were interested in Shijo and were posting their own Shijo translations online.

It should be difficult to translate highly culture-based lines of poetry, and I fear I might have done something wrong. Yet, I believe that it is a great honor and a fortune to introduce our marvelous legacy of culture to the world by myself. I do hope people all over the globe would enjoy and develop Shijo, revitalizing Shijo in the end.

Reflections

Park Jae Woo

I was a complete stranger to Shijo when Mr. Lee offered me a chance to take part in this project. I accepted it without much hesitation, maybe because it looked nice to take part in writing a book. Though the whole work has continued for about two years, I do not think it has been a time-consuming burden. I really enjoyed the translation itself and felt kind of proud whenever my translation was added to the selected list. In all respects, I can say that I have gained a lot in this work, in cooperation with an aspiring teacher and clever friends.

First, I've got an ear and eye for poetry. These days, it seems to me, students in Korea show less interest in poetry than other branches of cultural activity like films and novels. They go to the movies, buy novels, but not a poetry book. Perhaps poetry is being considered just as one of the school subjects, rather than a kind of cultural activity to enjoy. I was exactly the same.

However, reading aloud, pondering over the meaning, and trying to feel the writer's feelings, it began to come to me, it sank deep into my heart, a kind of silent beauty of Shijo, as it were, the first real live experience to me in regard to poetry. Further, after translating Shijo into an English version, when I read it aloud with

English rhythm, I was thrilled. This thrilling experience has worked as the driving force for my creativity throughout the long work.

My favorite Shijo is the one by Yi Jo-nyern.

> Moon breaks white on pear blossoms
> and milky-way reaches into midnight.
> The night bird, how could it know
> the feel of the coming spring hidden in a branch?
> I could not,
> sleep a wink, even a wink tonight,
> as if it were an illness, the sensitivity to me.

The biggest appeal of Shijo lies perhaps in its rhythm. It's only after I translated this Shijo above that I recognized the beauty in Shijo. Of course the beauty revealed itself when I was reading aloud. The beautiful lyrics combined with the rhythm of Shijo touched my heart. Especially the 3-5-4-3 rhythm in the third Line. It fascinated me. After this Shijo, my interest gained momentum. My first draft of the translation of this Shijo, which is as follows, did not survive.

> Moon breaks / white on pear
> Milk's dropped / in mid air
> How could / an owl know
> Feeling of / coming spring
> I could not
> Sleep a wink tonight
> For the tenderness / like a fever

I like this Shijo for its beautiful and dreamy lyrics. On the other hand, the following is, personally, my best translation, <Reed> by Ban Yung Ho.

꽃인 듯
꽃도 아닌 꽃을
꽃처럼 피웠구나

Like a flower,
you blossomed a flower
which isn't a flower shaped like a flower.

This time, my first draft survives into this book, untouched. Though it's a one-Lined Shijo, it was much more difficult to translate than any other three-Lined pyerng-Shijo. I figured it was the point in this Shijo, the alliteration of the word, 'flower'(꽃), which appears four times at the beginning of each segment. So, I rhymed the word, 'flower', at the end of each segment. I can still vividly remember how glad I was after finishing this one.

I also feel that translating Shijo improved my English significantly. I mean I learned some sense of English, rather than some specific knowledge. In the process of making the lines longer and shorter to make them fit into the rhythm, I picked up some intuition for making long sentences short. As we all know, essential elements of poetry are ellipsis and condensation, which is not easy to do properly. It requires precise and deeper knowledge of grammar and also some sense of English. As long as it makes sense, the shorter, the better. And writing poetry in English would be the best way to practice ellipsis and condensation. I think I've gathered some strength to write good English sentences.

Following is my translation, inspired by Mr. Lee's idea when I got stuck and was trying to find a good expression. It's a poem titled, <Pleasure and Agony> written by Kim So-werl.

Sweet or sour's in the mouth
먹이의 달고 씀은 입에 달리고

Success or failure's in the mind
영욕의 苦와 樂도 맘에 달렸소

It is a much better expression than 'A depend on B'. 'A be in B', this will be the best simple expression for the meaning 'A가 B에 달렸다.' Omitting 'whether' clauses from 'Whether it's sweet or sour' or 'Whether it's success or failure', then there cannot be simpler nor more to the point expression. There seems to be some obvious difference of level in English knowledge, between 'It depends on the mouth whether it's sweet or sour' and 'sweet or sour's in the mouth.'

And following is another part in the same poem.

Don't be looking only your steps
기구한 발뿌리만 보지 말고서

There should be no problem in omitting 'at' out of 'look at', because it will make sense to anyone. Someone could say it is grammatically wrong, but I prefer the rhythmic simplicity.

Following is a part of <No title 1> by Yi Young-do

Two of us with weary hearts
서루 야위 가슴

would only look out the window.
먼 창만 바라다가

'먼 창만 바라다가' means looking far out of the window. At first, I was embarrassed that my translation was too long over and over. The shortest one, to my best, had been something like 'Look out of the window', with 'Far' removed. But when I also omitted 'of', it became better. I had been thinking that 'out' and 'of' should always come together. I learned that sometimes it can be more concise and be conveyed more precisely when 'of' is removed.

Looking for the exact word among many synonyms, I could learn about precise meanings and nuances of lots of English words. Especially in poetry which consists of short-but-thick sentences, I had to put my whole energy into the choice of words. I mean, it had to be more precise and more condensed because it was shorter. And through making a distinction between formal and informal words, I could learn lots of informal words which are used in poetry. Understanding words' nuances really improved my English.

Also, through contemplating whether or not my sentence would make sense to native speakers and trying to revise it over and over, I could develop some sense of English. It was surprising that there are some English expressions which are understood only by Coreans, not by native speakers. And more surprising was that I had been using that kind of expressions so easily. We can refer to it as 'Conglish'. I was glad to fix my 'Conglish' one by one. Overall, I feel this process of translation has upgraded my English very much.

Besides English study, I had a great opportunity to learn more deeply about our Shijo. Especially so for me, who at first was put in charge of writing the introduction part of this book. It was so great an experience to do research into Shijo by myself, researching the related books in the library, surfing the internet both domestic and international, and so on. Also, I got confidence in the Shijo part of the school curriculum because in this project we covered almost all the Shijo mentioned in the high school level. I remember that even when preparing for the school examination, unlike other students, I did not have to spend very much time in Shijo.

Above all, however, it was a real pleasure to have an opportunity to study beyond high school level. Especially for me, who was initially responsible for writing the introduction for this book. It was a good experience. The introduction part of this book, intended to present a framework, fundamental principles and rules of 'Shijo in English', is without doubt, the most important part.

I had to present the definition of 'Shijo in English', but it was not that easy. I had to understand precisely the basic rules and definition of the original Corean Shijo, I also had to have my own view, and come up with some ideas which can help the original attraction of Shijo preserved and emphasized even in English, and also which would add some new flavor when English is combined. Following are what Mr. Lee suggests in the book.

1) Use the word 'Line' with a capital 'L' to mean one of the first, second, and third line of the poem.

2) Use the word 'FSTL' and 'SSTL', shortened from 'the first segment of the third Line' and 'the second segment of the third Line'. It is also because those two are so meaningful in Shijo that it is necessary to employ new terms for them.

3) The basic format of Shijo is seven-lined, which means each of the three Lines is separated into two, and then FSTL and SSTL separate once again from each other (which makes one more line), to expose the rhythm better.

4) In English Shijo, FSTL does not have to be three-syllabled. It need not be in patterned phrase, either, like exclamation or something(The reason is well explained in the intro).

In the introduction, there is a clear definition of 'Shijo in English'. I am sure that it will be the most reasonable and clear one among all other ones ever presented. I hope in the future lots of English Shijo are written in seven lines. I am so glad to have had a chance to try for the introduction of this book, though as our initial plan, each student being in charge of some part, mine the introductory part, was changed and Mr. Lee wrote the introduction himself.

I am glad to stand at the forefront of the work to introduce to the world our precious literature, Shijo. It was a blessing for me as a high school student to do something so worthwhile like this. During the whole work, I could see how real-life scholarly work gets done.

I'd like to express a big gratitude for my mother who stood by me during this project, Mr. Lee who trusted me and all friends who cooperated together.

Shijo is a unique poetry form which should be read being conscious of its origin, the song. It is charming enough to be able to touch deep into the world's heart. I think it just depends on our concern and effort. I am looking forward to the day when Shijo creates a sensation all around the world.

Part 5: Translation into Corean

참가자들

이경훈: 편집, Editor's Preface, Introduction
서울대학교 언어학과 졸업
서울대학교 법과대학 졸업

Amy Levine : Review
국립창원대학교 객원 교수

William Edwards: 영문 감수, 비판과 의견 제시, 후기
McMaster 대학교 영문학 & 문화학 석사
토론토 대학교 교육학 석사
전, 창원대 영문과 객원교수

김진묵: Foreword, Essay
음악평론가, 작곡가, 월드뮤직 전문가, 공연기획가

김온승 ; 김해 외국어 고등학교

박재우 ; 전 - 김해 외국어 고등학교

이정은 ; 용인 외국어 고등학교

한재은 ; 김해 외국어 고등학교

Introductory Notes

1. 'Korea'라고 표기하기 보다는 'Corea'라고 표기하는 것이 더 적당하다고 보아서, 'Corea'라고 표기하였다. 'Canada'라고 하지 않고 'Kanada'라고 쓰인다고 생각해보라.

2. 한국인의 이름은 성이 앞에 오고 이름이 뒤에 오게 적었다.

3. 영어 모국어인들은 'Shijo'를 단복수 모두를 의미하는 것으로 쓰고 있다. "three Shijo", "many Shijo"라는 표현이 쓰인다. 불가산으로 쓰인다면 한국에서 시조 한 수, 두 수 하듯이 영어로도 "a shoo of Shijo"라는 식으로 쓰는 것도 한가지 방법일 것이다. 이 책에서도 "Shijo"의 용법에 대하여 혼란이 조금 있다고 볼 수 있는데, 당분간 이런 혼란은 지속되리라 본다.

4. 대문자 'Line'은 시조의 초중종 3 장 중의 하나를 의미한다.

5. "arjirarng'yi"는 "arjirarng-yi"로 띄어서 발음한다는 표시다.

6. 이 책의 뒷부분에는 Review, Reflections, Foreword, Editor's Preface, Introduction, Epilogues의 번역이 실려있다. 원문의 맛을 독자들이 느낄 수 있게끔 직역하였다. 영문이 먼저 쓰인 다음 한글로 번역이 된 것이고, 영문과 한글이 따로 수정되기도 하였으므로 영문과 한글이 완전히 대응되지 않을 수 있다. 번역은 영문의 원 모습을 독자들이 느낄 수 있게끔 하기 위하여 직역하였다.

7. 어떤 시조의 번역은 편집자가 번역자로 표시되어 있다. 일부 학생들이 중간에 그만둔 경우 그 시조들 중에서 일부를 편집자가 처음부터 새로 번역하여 실었다.

< Review >

번역은 느리고 어려운 작업이지만 매우 풍성하고 보람 있는 일이기도 합니다. 저는 번역의 어려움을 지금까지 몇 번 경험했습니다만 제가 번역했던 시는 여기 학생들, 선생님, 그리고 부모님들이 애를 쓰신 시조처럼 복잡하지는 않았습니다. 저는 이 책이 얼마나 큰 성취인가를 알 수 있을만큼만 공감할 수 있을 뿐입니다. 이 책을 펼치면 나오는 보석들에 대해서 구체적인 통찰을 줄 수 있을 정도는 유감스럽게도 아니지요. 이런 제한 속에서나마 몇 마디 드리고자 합니다.

우선 한 언어의 행태와 그 언어의 토속적인 표현들을 배우는 데는 그 언어로 쓰인 시를 번역해보는 것 보다 더 좋은 방법이 없다는 것입니다. 이 책처럼 모국어에서 외국어로 번역하는 경우는 더욱 그러하지요. 둘째로 여기에 나온 시조의 이미지, 감성은 번역에 나타난 원 시조에 대한 번역자 나름대로의 시야를 보여주고 있다는 것입니다. 번역된 시조마다에 원래 시조에 의심할 바 없이 있었을 사연과 같은 정도의 많은 사연이 있었음을 느낄 수 있었습니다. 마지막으로 여기에 영어로 쓰인 시조의 구조는 원 시조의 시인과 번역자가 같이 어우러져서 우아하게 춤을 추는 듯한 예술성을 보여주고 있다는 것입니다. 겉으로 보기에 막힘이 없고 활짝 열린 듯이 보이지만 조용한 절제와 테크닉이 있습니다. 시조는 탱고만큼이나 복잡합니다.

이 점을 염두에 두고서 저는 독자들이 이 책에 수록된 예술작품을 정독하고, 읽고 다시 또 읽으시라고 초대합니다. 이 책에는 기뻐할 만한 것들이 매우 많습니다. 이 일을 끝까지 같이 해내신 학생들과 선생님 그리고 가족에게 축하의 인사를 보냅니다. 시조라는 아름다운 예술형식을 영어로 번역해주심에 감사드립니다.

Amy Levine

국립 창원대학교

영어영문학과 객원교수

존경받는 영국시인 존 키이츠는 시 창작을 나무에서 싹이 돋아나는 것에 비유한 적이 있다. - 시는 자연발생적으로 흘러나오지 않을 거라면, 차라리 나오지 않는 것이 낫다. 낭만적인 이 비유에는 시는 그 시가 그렇게 나올 수 밖에 없는 뭔가가 있다는 확신이 들어있다. 키이츠는 좋은 시는 어린 나무를 어르고 달래서 추운 겨울에 싹을 틔우게 할 수 없듯이, 머리를 굴려서 쓸 수 있는 것이 아니라고 믿었다. 키이츠에게 시는 자연적으로 나와서 - 내면에 감춰져 있던 시가 용출하여 남들이 알지 못하는 자기만의 존재의 이유로 세상에 존재해야만 했다.

이 한국시조의 영어번역을 읽었을 때, 여기 포함된 시조들 중 빛나는 시적 절제의 아름다움을 가진 일부 시조들은 충격이었다. 고시조 중에서 특히 서익의 시조는 시적절제의 웅대함, 중국 전설의 풍부한 활용, 시에 생명을 불어넣고 있는 갈망 때문에 특히 관심이 갔다:

이 뫼를 헐어내어 저 바다를 메우면은
봉래산(蓬萊山) 고운 님을 걸어가도 보련마는
이 몸이 정위조(精衛鳥) 같아야 바자닐만 하노라.

서 익 (1542-1587)

이 시는 뉘앙스가 풍부하고, 사람의 눈길을 잡아끄는 힘이 있다. “바다 앞에서” 서성이는 이미지는 시인으로 하여금 욕망의 대상에 이르지 못하게 하는, 어찌해볼 수 없는 장애물을 나타내고 있다; 그런 뜻 외에도 “앞에서”는 바다가, 지리적인 경계들이 있기 이전부터 이미 있었던 변함 없는 갈망 상태를 나타내는 시간 표지를 뜻하기도 한다. 이렇게 이 시는 번역을 통하여 뉘앙스가 더 풍부해졌는데, 영어에서 “before"라는 전치사가 “특정한 시간의 이전”을 의미하기도 하고, “특정한 공간의 앞”을 의미하기도 하는 이중적 의미를 갖고 있기 때문이다.

이 시는 미아가 되어서 새로 화했다는 딸에 얽힌 중국의 전설을 배경으로 하고 있다. 아버지는 신인데, 필사적으로 딸을 찾는다; 그렇지만 그 아이는 자기가 죽었다는 걸 모르고, 바다를 건너가서 아버지를 만나기 위해서 계속 바다를 메우려고 한다. 조선시대의 많은 시조는 왕을 찬양하는 시조였다.

이 시의 배경이 되고 있는, 미아가 된 딸에 얽힌 중국의 전설은 불가능한 일, 즉, 다시 왕을 만나고 싶은 시인의 갈망과 의지를 상징하고 있다. 이렇게 모멘텀을 축적한 시는 산의 모래로 바다를 메우는 불가능한 일을 해내는 환상을 꿈꾸고 있는 대상(역주: 새를 말함)의 존재를 인지하면서 창의적으로 나아간다. 드라마틱한 반전은 여기에 나온다: “But I am". 인간 한계에 대한 이 인식은 긍정적인 만큼이나 절망적이기도 하다. 시인은 아버지를 잃은 딸이 아버지와 멀리 있는 만큼 왕으로부터 신화적으로 멀어져 있다.

이 한국시조집을 대했을 때, 내게 일어났던 주된 감정은 다음 두 가지였다. 우선, 호기심에 사로잡혔다. 이 독특한 시 형식을 내가 들어보지 못했던 이유가 알고 싶어졌다. 다양한 문화권의 문학을 공부했기 때문에, 한국 시에 대한 무지는 내 마음을 불편하게 했다. 실제로 비교문학 코스에서 일본의 하이쿠와 다른 동양의 시를 접했음을 기억한다. 선불교와 선불교의 공안(公案)도 공부했다. 그렇지만 내가 캐나다에서 학사, 석사를 할 때 한국 시조는 커리큘럼에 한 번도 없었다.

슬프게도, 한국 시조는 그리 알려져 있지 못하다. 한국 시조는 서양학자들의 관심을 끌지 못했다; 그렇지만 지금은 변하고 있을지도 모른다. 이 괜찮은 한국시조의 번역에 즈음하여 기대되는 것은 이 책이 독특하고 풍부한 시적인 형태에 대한 관심을 불러일으켜서 강력한 전설에 대하여 그리고 시조를 구성하는 주제들(역주: 충성, 우정, 사랑 등)에 대하여 더 깊은 연구가 이어지는 것이다.

언어 구사에서의 압축, 전설과 고사의 활용, [종장에서의] 주제의 반전은 한국의 시조에 독특한 특질을 부여하여 시조 읽기가 기쁨이 되게 한다.

시의 창작을 나무에 이파리가 돋듯이 자연스러운 것으로 생각해본다면, 이 책은 오랜 전통을 가진 한국 시조에 대한 가장 최근의 기여로서 이 예술 형식이 아직도 꽃을 피워내고 있음을 보여주고 있다. 이 번역에 애를 쓴 이경훈과 네 명의 떠오르는 학자들은 좋은 시에 영어로 생명을 부여하는 찬사를 받을 만한 일을 해냈다.

William Edwards

McMaster 대학교 영문학 & 문화학 석사

토론토 대학교 교육학 석사

전, 창원대 영어영문학과 객원교수

< Foreword >

슬픈 노래, 삶에서 가장 아름다운

Sadness, most beautiful moment of Life

노래를 하지 않고 어떻게
살 수 있을까
슬픈 노래가 더욱
깊이 다가오는 것은 무슨 까닭일까
삶이
본질적으로 슬픈 것이기 때문일까

노래를 하지 않고 어떻게
살 수 있을까 우리는

사람들은 어찌할 수 없는 것을 노래한다. 아니, 어찌할 수 없기에 노래한다. 결국 모든 노래가 한정된 삶을 이야기한다. 어쩌면 한정된 삶이기에 노래를 하는 것인지도 모른다.

●

노래는 메시지이다. 그렇기에 인간의 내면을 두드리는 노래는 영원이 메아리친다. 우리 선조들은 시조라는 형식에 메시지를 담았다. 메시지를 담아낼 때면 감정을 극명하게 드러내지 않는다. 감정은 숨길수록 깊어지고 드러내면 천해지기 때문이다. 허허로운 분위기 속에 감정을 숨기는 것에 시조의 묘미가 있다. 깊이 숨길수록 마지막의 반전(反轉)이나 상승(上昇) 효과가 커진다. 그래서 선조들의 노래를 들으면 고개를 끄덕이거나 무릎을 치게 된다. 때로는 엄청난 파괴력으로 다가오기도 한다.

정몽주와 이방원이 술잔을 마주하고 앉았다. 술이 한 순배 돌자 이방원이 노래한다.

이런들 어떠하리 저런들 어떠하리
만수산 드렁칡이 얽혀진들 어떠하리
우리도 이같이 얽혀 백년까지 누리리라

유명한 '하여가'(何如歌)이다. 그는 만수산을 손짓으로 가리키며 다 같이 어울려 사는 삶을 노래한다. 그러나 본 뜻은 고려가 망하고 이조가 세워졌으니 새로운 세상에서 어울려 살자는 유혹의 노래이다. 이방원은 권력을 나누어갖자는 간교한 이야기를 하고 있다. 고려의 충신 정몽주는 죽음을 예감한다. 그리고 빙그레 웃으며 화답하는 노래를 부른다.

이 몸이 죽고 죽어 일백번 고쳐 죽어
백골이 진토되어 넋이라도 있고 없고
님 향한 일편단심 가실 줄이 있으랴

이 역시 유명한 '단심가'(丹心歌)이다. 노래를 통해 주군을 배신하고 나라를 차지한 이들과 함께 할 수 없다고 단호하게 거절한 것이다. 그리고 술자리가 끝나고 돌아가다가 선죽교에서 이방원의 부하들에게 죽음을 맞는다.

●

미국의 흑인들은 블루스(Blues)를 노래한다. 노예에서 해방되어 도시의 빈민이 된 흑인들, 아무런 보호 장치 없는 사회의 밑바닥에서 생존해야하는 이들, 범죄와 수감생활을 반복하며 삶을 사는 사람들의 노래가 블루스였다.

이 블루스가 우리의 시조와 흡사한 구조를 지니고 있다는 사실은 경이롭다. 흑인들은 삶의 고달픔을 독특한 3행시로 노래했다. 이 시가가 후에 음악으로의 블루스가 된다. 우리의 시조도 음악으로 연주될 때에는 시조창(唱 Shijo-as-song)이 된다.

음악에서의 블루스는 4박 4소절이 1행이 되어 모두 12소절(segment) 형태로 노래된다. 시조 역시 4개의 음운이 1행으로 된 3행구조로 되어 있다. 그래서 시조를 블루스 12소절에 맞추어 노래하면 딱 맞아 떨어진다. 단어하나, 음운하나 남거나 부족하지 않다.

블루스는 삶의 고통이 피워낸 인류의 자산이다. 흑인들의 아픔이 컸기에 노래와 반주 혹은 기악형태로 나타난 블루스의 호소력도 크다. 20세기에 태어난 블루스는 그 처절한 기운으로 세계인을 매료시켰다. 우리나라의 대중음악에도 큰 영향을 주었다. 옛가요에서부터 현재의 알앤비까지 많은 노래들이 흑인들의 블루스를 모태로 하고 있다.

우리민족이 수수천년을 노래한 시조에는 기다림과 그리움이 담겨있다. 나는 격하지 않고 감정을 깊이 감춘 우리의 노래가 21세기 세계음악의 큰 부분을 차질할 것을 예견한다. 느림의 미학이 삶의 미덕으로 인식되는 시대, 짧은 3행시가 10분 넘게 노래되는 시조창에 그 열쇠가 있다. 우리의 시조 역시 고귀한 인류의 자산이다.

김 진 묵(음악평론가)

< Artistic class, humane scent and taste of Old Pops >

김 진 묵

문화가 산책
옛가요의 예술적 격조와 인간적 향취

문학소년 시절 라이너 마리아 릴케를 좋아했다. 그의 명상시집 '두이노의 비가'에 심취했다. 릴케는 소년 시절에 '나는 언젠가 봄에 죽으리라'고 노래했다. 나도 언젠가 봄에 죽고 싶다고 생각했다. 문학은 물론 클래식 음악도 나를 매료시켰다. 슈베르트도 좋아했고, 말러와 볼프의 가곡도 좋아했다.

반면에 우리 문화에 대해서는 부정적인 생각이 깊었다. 현인이 '굳세어라 금순아'에서 '♬ 이 내 몸은 국제시장 장사치기다 ♪' 하고 노래할 때는 화가 났다. 너무 원색적이고 유치하다는 생각이 들었다. 그러나 나이에 따라 삶의 준엄함을 겪으면서 생각이 달라지기 시작했다. 생존의 몸부림 속에서 잃어버린 가족을 그리는 처절한 노래임을 알았기 때문이다. 특히 '♩영도다리 난간 위에 초생달만 외로이 떴다 ♬'라는 부분은 눈물 없이 들을 수 없다. 전화(戰禍)를 피해 급히 피난을 가며, 부산에서 만나기로 하고 말로만 듣던 '영도다리에서 만나자' 하고 소리치던 사람들이 모여들어 영도다리는 피난민들의 이산가족 찾는 장소가 되었다. 그러나 저녁이 되어 초승달이 떴는데도 그리운 사람은 나타나지 않았다.

옛 가요에는 우리의 아픈 근세사가 녹아 있다. 나라 잃은 슬픔과 동족 사이의 전쟁 그리고 남존여비 사상으로 아픔을 겪은 여성들의 한이 내재되어 있다. 민요가 20 세기에 이르러 신민요를 낳았고, 서양음악이 들어오며 가요가 되는 역사 속에 민족의 정서는 숨쉬고 있었다. 반면 요즘 노래는 발라드와 R&B 등 흑인음악 정서로 일관하고 있다. 이러한 사회현상에 대한 우려의 목소리도 높다.

지난 11월 2일 저녁 충무로의 ‘한국의 집’에서 옛 가요를 사랑하는 사람들이 모인 ‘유정천리’(회장: 이동순 영남대 국문학과 교수)의 창립대회가 있었다. 옛 가요의 예술적 격조와 인간적 향취를 위한 조촐한 상을 차린 것이다. 일부 부정적 시각으로 온당한 평가를 받지 못하고 있는 옛 가요의 위상을 재확립하기 위해 시인, 법조인, 방송인, 문화인, 국회의원, 공무원 등 다양한 계층의 사람들이 모여 우리 옛 가요의 가치를 재확인하기에 이르렀다.

‘가련다 떠나련다 어린 아들 손을 잡고’로 시작하는 박재홍의 노래 ‘유정천리(有情千里)에서 이름을 딴 이 모임은 다양한 사업을 계획하고 있다. 축음기 콘서트, 옛 가요 명인과의 만남, 학술대회, 자료전시회, 박물관 건립 등을 추진한다. 12월 중순 경, 예술의 전당 예술정보관 3층 공동감상실 심포니에서 '소녀의 꿈', ‘홍콩 아가씨’ 등을 불렀던 금사향 선생을 모시고 축음기 콘서트, 옛 가요 명인과의 만남 행사를 갖는다.

< Editor's Preface >

이 책은 한국시조를 단순한 영어로의 번역이 아닌 영어시조로 번역하고자 했다. 번역에는 네 명의 학생이 참가했다. 이런 과정을 거쳤다. 필자가 번역할 한글 시조 목록을 정했다. 학생들은 목록에서 맘에 드는 시조를 선택하여 번역한 것을 보내왔다. 같은 시조에 대한 여러 번역이 제출되었을 때는 그 중에서 가장 잘 된 것을 선정했다. 제출된 번역이 처음부터 일정한 정도의 수준에 이르지 못한 경우는, 하나의 시조에 대한 번역을 한 학생만 제출한 경우에도 선정에서 제외되었다. 이런 방식으로 우리는 시조를 번역할 학생을 선정했다.

어떤 경우에는 제출한 번역이 별다른 수정의 필요가 없이 막바로 채택이 되는 경우도 있었다. 그렇지 않은 경우에는 학생들의 번역을 살펴보고 의견을 붙여서 돌려보냈다. 많은 경우에 이런 오고감은 아주 여러 번 계속해야만 했었다. 학생들의 번역을 가급적 고치지 않으려고 했기 때문이다. 나는 일정한 거리를 두고, 다음과 같은 의견만을 말하려고 했다; “이 단어는 너무 딱딱하다”, “이 표현은 너무 직설적이다”, “음수율이 안맞다” 등등. 그렇게 하지 않으면 학생들의 번역이 아니라 나의 번역이라고 봐야할 것이기 때문이다. 학생들은 제출한 번역이 의견이 붙어서 돌아올 때마다, 번역이 다 된 것으로 채택될 때까지는 인내심의 한계를 시험당하는 느낌을 받았을 것이다. 이에 그들의 노력과 인내심에 깊은 경의를 표한다.

처음에 우리는 시조에 대해서, 시조의 영어번역에 대해서는 더욱 더 잘 몰랐었다. 이 일이 그렇게 호락호락한 일이 아니라는 걸 알았다면 시작을 아니했었을 것이다. 어떻든 우리는 만났고 같이 공부했는데 그 과정에서, 그리고 시간이 흘러감에 따라서 우리는 시조와 시조의 영어번역에 대해서 점점 더 알아가게 되었다. 우리는 점점 시조의 구조, 영어시조의 바람직한 모습에 대해서 감을 잡아가기 시작했다. 우리는 FSTL, SSTL 그리고 시조 배열 형식에 대해서 조금씩 알게 되었다.

고시조만 번역하기로 했었지만 이 책에는 현대시조도 번역되어 있다. 시조가 아닌 자유시도 일부 포함되어 있는데 이 작품들은 시조작가의 작품이거나 시조와 밀접한 관련이 있는 작가의 작품이다. 예를 들어, 유희경의 한시들은 그가 이매창의 연인이었기 때문에 포함되었다. 3 편에는 잘 알려진 한국인의 애송시가 번역되어 있다.

이호우 시조시인과 그 여동생인 이영도 시조시인의 작품 번역에 대한 허락 과정에서 많은 애를 써주신 유명한 화가이시자 시조시인인 민병도 시인께 깊은 감사를 드린다. 단장 시조집 "퇴화의 날개"에 실려 있는 단장시조의 번역을 허락해주신 반영호 시인께 깊은 감사를 드린다. 반영호 시인의 단장시조는 현대시 편에 있다.

네 학생들의 부모님께도 깊이 감사를 드린다. 부모님들은 오랜 동안 우리를 말 없이 지지해주셨고, 정신적으로 경제적으로 지원을 아끼지 않으셨으며, 우리가 약해졌을 때 힘을 주셨고 이 책이 나오기까지 변함 없이 기다려주셨다. 그 분들의 헌신이 없었더라면 이 책은 가능하지 않았을 것이다.

유명한 음악평론가, 작곡가, 공연기획가, 음악 칼럼니스트, 그리고 월드뮤직 전문가이신 김진묵 선생이 서문을 써주신 것은 우리에게 대단한 영광이다. 김진묵 선생은 한국 최초의 재즈 평론가이시고, 전세계의 여러 음악 즉 월드뮤직에 정통하시기로 잘 알려져 계신, 민속음악 혹은 종족음악의 전문가시다. 우리의 감사를 표하기 위하여 선생의 블로그 http://cafe.naver.com/carvonism.cafe/에 올라와 있는 에세이 중에서 한 편을 번역해서 실었다. 그 에세이는 Foreword 다음에 나온다.

리바인 교수가 추천사를 써주신데 대해서 우리 모두는 깊은 감사를 드린다. 리뷰에서 우리는 리바인 교수가 그리 길지 않은 기간 동안임에도 불구하고 시조의 깊은 면을 꿰뚫으신 것 같다는 느낌을 받았다. 추천사는 우리가 무엇을 하고자 했는지 우리가 독자들에게 뭘 읽고, 뭘 느끼고, 뭘 즐기기를 원했는지를 잘 안다고 우리를 안심시키는 듯이 보인다. 리바인 교수가 시간이 부족해서 더 많은 조언을 듣지 못한 것을 애석하게 생각한다.

학생들, 부모님들 그리고 나는 윌리엄 에드워즈 선생께 가슴 깊은 곳에서 우러나는 감사를 드린다. 에드워즈 선생은 영어 원어민 교정을 봐주셨고, 귀한 의견을 주셨고, 후기까지 써주셨다. 구석구석 치밀하게 빼놓지 않고 봐주셨고, 오타도 찾아주셨다. 우리의 일이 선생의 의견과 후기로 인하여 더 크고 더 깊은 것으로 변모해가는 것을 보는 것은 놀라운 경험이었다. 개인적으로는 선생의 프로페셔널한 일에 깊은 감명을 받았다. 그리고 선생의 코멘트를 받은 후에 Introduction을 새로 썼음을 고백한다. 코멘트를 받은 후에 조금 추가한 부분도 있고, 약간 고친 부분도 있기 때문에 문법적 오류가 있을 수도 있다고 본다. 만약 하나라도 있다면, 그 오류는 나의 것이다.

영어 시조의 연구에 많은 노력을 기울이신 교수들과 학자들에게 감사드린다. 그분들의 논문을 읽으면서 지식과 식견을 쌓을 수 있었다. 그런 선행 연구가 없었더라면, 이 책은 크게 의미가 없는 그저 또 하나의 시조번역책에 불과했었을 것이다.

우리는 이 책이 한국 문화와 한국인 정서의 깊은 곳에 관심을 가진 외국인들에게 조금이나 도움이 되기를 바란다. 고시조든 현대시조든 시조를 읽으면 한국과 한국인을 매우 잘 이해하게 된다고 우리는 믿는다. 우리가 이 책을 내는 과정에서 얻게 된 것들이 영어시조에 관심이 있는 분들께 도움이 되었으면 한다. 중학생이나 고등학생들도 이 책을 읽으면서 시조와 영어에 대해서 도움을 받을 수 있기를 기대한다. 영어시조 또는 영어에 관심 있는 분들의 아낌 없는 조언과 꾸짖음을 기대하며, 이메일로 의견을 보내주신다면 매우 고맙게 받겠다.

메일: taran707@gmail.com 또는 taran707@naver.com

< Introduction >

(이하에서 마디 또는 토막이라 하는 것은 영어의 segment에 대응하는 것이며, 이는 시조의 초중종장의 한 장을 넷으로 나눈 것을 의미합니다).

세부로 들어가기 전에 약간 맛을 좀 보기로 하자. 아래에 시조 한 수가 일곱 줄로 배열되어 있고 각 줄은 두 토막(segment)으로 되어 있다.

Having left my fair lord,
far away and far apart,
I sat alone at a stream,
'cause I had nowhere to put my heart.
The water there,
must be like my heart, walking
along the dark path, sobbing and weeping.

우선 어떻게 읽는지를 보자. 이렇게 읽어야 한다. "//" 표시된 곳에서 끊어 읽는다.

Having left // my fair lord,
far away // and far apart,
I sat alone // at a stream,
'cause I had nowhere // to put my heart.
The water there, //, //, //
must be like my heart walking
along the dark path, // sobbing and weeping.

시조 전체는 12 토막(segment)으로 나뉘어져 있음을 알 수 있다. 각 토막을 읽는 시간은 같다. "The water there" 다음에는 "//"가 세 개 표시되어 있다. 여기서 다른 곳에서 쉴 때 보다 더 오래 쉬라는 뜻이다. 여섯째 줄, "must be like my heart, walking"은 다른 토막 보다 더 길면서도 "//" 표시가 없다. 이는 이 토막은 중간에 쉬지 말고 망서림 없이 단숨에 그리고 약간 서둘러서 다른 토막을 읽는 것과 같은 시간 내에 읽어야 함을 의미한다. 크게 소리 내어 읽으면, 어떤 리듬이나 박자가 느껴질 것이다. 그 리듬감, 박자감이 시조의 특질이다. 그리고 여섯째 줄은 더 길지만, 중간에 쉬지 않고 다른 토막을 읽을 때와 같은 시간 내에 읽어야 한다는 것은 시조의 필수불가결한 요소다.

Why a new one?

시조가 무엇인지는 한국사람이라면 대체로 알고 있을 것이다. 깊은 이론적인 것이야 전문학자들이나 안다 하더라도, 한 두 수의 시조를 흥얼거리지 못하는 한국 사람은 없을 것이고, 아주 경계선상에 놓인 최근의 일부 첨단의 현대시조가 아닌 한은, 이것이 시조인가 아닌가를 구분하지 못하는 사람도 없을 것이다.

문제는 영어시조다. 한국의 시조가 일본의 하이쿠에 비하여 덜 알려진 가장 큰 이유가 홍보부족, 정부의 노력부족이라고 하지만, 그 보다는, 그 형식에 있어서, "이것이 시조다"라는 걸 제시하여 주지 못한 것이 아닌가 한다. 서구인들의 웹사이트 시조동호회에 가보면, 시조가 정확히 무엇인지, 어디까지가 시조이고 어디까지가 아닌지에 대해서 갈증을 느끼고 있는 듯이 보인다. 예를 들어, 우리는 시조의 한 장이 홀수로 예를 들어, 세 토막이나 다섯 토막으로 나뉘어질 수 있다고는 생각하지 않는다. 우리는 그것을 시조로 보지 않는다. 그러나 서구인들은 그렇게 써놓고 시조라고 생각하는 경우도 본다.

우리는 종장에서의 반전이 뭘 의미하는지도 잘 알고 있다. 종장의 첫 구 다음 구는 다른 구보다 더 길어져야 한다는 것, 그렇지만 그 보다 더 짧은 구가 발음되는 것과 같은 시간 내에 발음이 되어야 한다는 것, 이래야만 시조다운 맛이 난다는 것 그리고 그것이 없으면 시조라고 보기도 어렵다는 것을 알고 있다.

그렇다면 영어로 번역된 시조, 영어로 쓰인 시조에서도 그런 시조의 맛이 나는가? 유감스럽게도 그렇지 못한 것이 현실이다. 현재의 영어시조, 영어로 번역된 시조는, 세 줄로 쓰인 영시와 별 차이가 없다. "세 줄로 된 영시와 과연 다른가?" 하는 질문에 답을 제시하지 못하는 한, 영어 시조는 없다. 이 책은 이런 문제점에 우리 나름대로의 해결책을 제시하고 있다. 물론 이 책이 필요한 모든 답을 주는 것은 아닐 것이다. 우리는 전문학자들의 더 나은 연구를 기대한다. 시간이 더 흐르고 나면, 영어시조에 대한 기본 이론이 정립되고 난 후에는, 영어시조는 영어를 쓰는 사람들이 하기 나름일 것이다. 그 때는 영어시조는 제 갈 길을 갈 것이고, 어디를 가고 있을 지는 우리가 지금 알 수 없는 것이다.

About Shijo

한국은 최소한 5천년이 넘는 오래된 나라이므로 문화유산이 다양한데 그 중의 하나가 시조다. 시조의 기원은 아무리 느리게 잡아도 14 세기, 고려시대(AD 918 ~ 1392) - 거기서 "Corea"라는 나라 이름이 나왔다 - 까지는 거슬러 올라가는 것으로 받아들여지고 있다. 한국문학사에 나타났던 시가 형식 중에서 시조만이 살아남아서 창작과 출판이 이루어지고 있다. 최신의 시조사전인 1991년도 간행, 박을수 편 시조대사전에는 5492 수의 시조가 수록되어 있다.

다른 형식은 예를 들어 가사인 경우, 완전히 죽은 것이 아니라 지금도 쓰여지고 있긴 하지만 문학적인 업적으로 평가되지는 않는다. 그래서 시조 시인은 있지만 가사 시인은 없다. 가사도 시조처럼 음악반주로 공연되었었다. 시조는 단가, 가사는 장가라 했다.

가사도 음보율 또는 음수율이 요구되고, 3+4 음절의 반복이라는 점에서는 시조와 같지만 다음에서 다르다; (1) 시조가 운문이며 시가의 한 형식임에는 의문의 여지가 없다. 가사는 운율이 있으니 산문은 아니다. 그렇다고 운문으로 단정하기도 어렵다. 운문의 형식으로 쓰여진 산문이다. 성경을 가사로 다시 쓴다면 좋은 예가 될 것이다. (2) 시조가 3장으로 제한되는데 반하여, 가사는 그런 제한이 없다. 가사는 40 장 또는 그 이상으로 길어질 수 있다. 시조는 3 장 이내에서 절제하지만 가사는 할 말을 다한다. (3)

협의의 시조는 종장에서의 반전이 있어야 하지만 가사는 꼭 그래야 하는 것은 아니다. 윤선도의 유명한 40수 연시조, 어부사시사는 40수를 묶어서 하나의 가사로 분류되기도 한다.

어떤 사람들은 가사를 부활시키자는 주장을 하기도 한다. 임종찬은 "현대시조의 진로모색과 세계화 문제 연구, 2005"라는 논문에서 "가사문학을 현대문학의 한 장르로 복원할 필요가 있다고 본다. 없애기에는 너무 아깝다고 생각한다"라고 밝히고 있다.

시조도 시조를 부활시키자는 주장을 누군가가 했고, 사람들이 동조해서 된 것이니 가사도 언젠가 부활될 지도 모른다. 시조가 날렵하고 잘빠진 젊은 여자라면, 가사는 능수능란하고 사교성 좋은 중년 남자일 것이다. 시조는 작가 개인의 내면의 감정이 직접 또는 간접으로 드러나야 하지만 가사에서는 반드시 그럴 필요는 없다. 그래서 가사는 정치적, 종교적, 교육적인 것을 쓰는 데 좋을 것이다. 시조와 가사를 남녀의 차이에 비유하는 것은 필자가 들어본 적이 없는 것인데 아마추어인 필자가 두 개의 서로 다른 전통 문학의 장르에 대해서 느끼는 개인적인 감정이라는 것을 독자들이 유의해주셨으면 한다. 이 비유는 (1) 시조는 개인적 감정을 표출하지만 가사는 반드시 그럴 필요가 없다는 것, (2) 시조는 종장에서의 반전이 필요하지만 가사는 그럴 필요가 없다는 것에 초점을 둔 것이다.

The word 'Shijo'

'Sijo'라고 쓰이기도 한다. 우리가 'Shijo'를 채택한 것은 'sh'가 'sea'의 's'처럼 경음으로 발음되지 않고 'sleep'의 's'처럼 부드럽게 발음되게 하기 위해서다. '시'는 시간 또는 계절을 뜻한다. 따라서 시조는 '시간'의 '조'가 된다. '조'는 지금도 쓰이는 말이다. 한탄조, 자랑조라는 말이 쓰인다. 한국인은 '조'를 달리 쓰기도 한다. "이 시는 4.4.조다"라고 했을 때는 "이 시는 4음절 + 4음절"로 쓰였다는 말이 된다. 시조는 3.4.조의 시가다. '조'는 음악에서 쓰이기도 한다. 한국 전통음악도 장조와 단조가 있다. 평조(서양음악의 장조에 해당한다)와 계면조(서양음악의 단조에 해당한다)라 한다. 따라서

'시조'는 '시간'의 조, '계절'의 '조'다.

Definition

시조의 명확한 정의를 밝히기는 어렵다. 시조란 말이 의미하는 것이 한가지만이 아니기 때문이다. 시조는 시조로 쓰인 텍스트를 의미하기도 하고, 음악 반주에 맞춘 가곡창을 의미하기도 한다. 이를 Shijo-as-music 즉, 음악으로서의 시조라고 부를 수 있을 것이다. 심지어 가곡창에서 사용하는 음악의 멜로디를 뜻하기도 한다. 다른 이유가 또 있다. 시조에는 여러 종류가 있기 때문이다. 주로 다뤄지는 것은 평시조다. 평시조 외에 다른 시조도 가능한 것이라면, 시조란 과연 무엇일까? 이 질문에 답하기는 어렵다. 이런 의문이 일어나는 이유는 시조가 노래로 출발했기 때문이다. 그 의문은 음악으로서의 시조와 관련이 되어 있다.

여기서 깊이 다루기가 어려우므로 참고상 간단히 짚고 넘어가기로 한다. 가곡창은 시조를 음악반주에 맞춰서 부르는 걸 뜻하는데, 그 가사로는 다양한 것들이 있는데 심지어 중국 한시도 포함된다. 따라서 가곡창은 무엇이든 담을 수 있는 빈 그릇과 같다는 뜻이 된다. 그런 경우에는 시조가 무엇인가 하는 의문은 떠오르지 않는다. 이제 텍스트로서의 시조시가 음악으로부터 독립하였으므로 이 문제가 표면으로 떠오르게 된다. 음악으로서의 시조는 필자의 능력을 넘어서는 것이므로 주로 텍스트로서의 시조만, 그 중에서도 평시조만 다루기로 한다.

텍스트로서의 시조의 정의는 한국에서 가장 유명하고 가장 영향력이 큰 조동일 교수가 잘 요약하고 있다. 이하는 조동일 교수의 한국문학통사 제 2 권 187 면 이하의 내용을 필자가 영어로 번역한 것이다. 인용한 내용은 "[[ ]]"로 표시하고자 한다.

[[시조가 언제 생겼는가 하는 의문은 시조의 정의에 따라 다르게 해결된다. 모두 세 줄이고, 한 줄은 네 토막이며, 한 토막을 이루는 기준음절수가 4음절인 형식을 갖춘 노래를 시조라고 한다면, 그런 것은 일찍부터 있었다. 백제노래라고 여겨지는 정읍사나

고려속악가사인 만전춘별사에 그런 형식이 보인다. 현대시라고 쓴 작품에도 동일한 형식을 사용한 사례가 더러 있다. 그런 것은 네 토막 형식이 네 줄이면 더 잘 어울릴 것이 세 줄로 끝나는 변이형이어서 어느 때든지 있게 마련이고, 독자적인 특징을 가진 문학갈래라고 의식되지 않았다. 그래도 명칭이 필요해 '유사시조'라고 하자는 견해도 있으나 '광의의 시조'라고 일컫는 것이 마땅하다.

'광의의 시조'보다 한 가지 요건이 더 있어 셋째 줄 첫 토막은 기준음절수 미달인 2자나 3자이고, 둘째 토막은 기준음절수 초과인 5자나 6자인 것은 '협의의 시조'이다. 그런 특별한 장치를 사용해 네 줄까지 나아가지 않고 세 줄로 끝나게 하는 결속력을 부여했다. 자연의 소산인 광의의 시조'를 일부 개조한 인공의 창조물이 '협의의 시조'다. 그런데 개조 방식은 다섯 줄 향가의 다섯 번 째 줄 서두에 감탄구가 와서 결말이 긴장되게 하는 방법을 다시 사용했다.

...

그런데 고려후기의 작품은 작자가 여럿이고 작품도 많아 신빙성을 의심하고 마는 것이 능사가 아니다. 그 때 문학의 갈래체계의 전면적인 개편이 일어나 새로운 서정시가 출현했다고 적극적으로 해석하는 편이 타당하다.]]

위에서 본 조동일 교수의 정의는 평시조에 대한 것이다.

Structure

1. Fundamentals

12구 주의에서 기본 음절수는 3+4다. 3음절 다음에 4음절이 나온다. 이는 한국어가 말해지는 양식이다. 한국어는 극단적으로 단순하게 말한다면, 3+4의 언어다. 시조는, 기본적으로 3+4의 노래, 3+4의 반복이라고 요약될 수 있다. 종장에서 3+4가 3+5로 바뀌는 반전이 일어나고 그 다음은 3+4가 4+3으로 역전된다. 종장에서의 음절수 변화는, 오늘날 시조라고 불리는 협의의 시조에서는 필수임을 간과하지 말아야 한다. 종장에는 특별한 지위가 부여되고 있다. 종장에서 시조가 끝나기 때문에 종장에서의 의미에서의 반전은 반드시 필요하다. 이런 종장의 특별한 위치는 '종장에서의 반전'이라고 불려왔다.

평시조의 표준음절수는 다음과 같이 제시되고 있다:

	12 구 주의	6 구 주의
초 장	3 + 4 + 3 + 4	7+7
중 장	3 + 4 + 3 + 4	7+7
종 장	3 + 5 + 4 + 3	8+7

위에서 보았듯이 시조는 3줄로 되어 있고, 각 줄은 4 마디, 한 마디는 평균 4 음절로 되어 있으며, 세번째 줄의 첫째 마디는 3음절로 되어 있고, 세번째 줄의 둘째 마디는 반전을 위해서 4음절을 넘게 길어져 있는 정형시라고 이해되고 있다. 세번째 줄의 첫마디는 FSTL이라 하고 두번째 마디는 SSTL이라 부르기로 한다.

그런데 다른 주장도 있다. 김정화는 "시조의 형태적 특질(2003년 발표)"이라는 논문에서 아주 다른 그러나 주목할 만한 의견을 제시하고 있다.

[[(1) 시조는 3 장이 아니라 4 장으로 되어 있다. FSTL이 단일구로 이루어진 독립된 장이기 때문이다. 단일구는 향가에서 보이듯 한국 시가의 특징이다. (2) FSTL이 3음절로 되어야 한다는 이유는 없다. 3음절은 리듬상의 필요에 의한 것이지 피할 수 없는 시(詩) 이론 때문이 아니다. (3) SSTL이 기준음절수 초과라는 주장은 의미가 없게 된다. 하나의 구가 아니라 제4장의 첫 두 구이기 때문이다. (4) FSTL은 흔히 모음으로 끝나서 길게 발음하기 쉽게 때문에 독립된

장으로서의 자격이 있다.]]

이 이론은 매우 신선하고 흥미로우며 사고를 자극한다. 그러나 그 이론은 충분한 증거의 뒷받침을 받아야할 것이다. 살펴보건대... 우선 FSTL은 모음으로 끝나는가? 박을수 편 시조대사전에서 처음 100 수를 보면 19수의 시조가 모음으로 끝나지 않는다. 그렇다면 80% 정도가 된다. 한국 시조 역사상 최고의 고수로 치는 황진이의 시조를 보자. 현존하는 6 수의 시조 중에서 5 수의 시조가 FSTL이 모음으로 끝난다. 83%가 된다. 그러므로 대략 80% 정도의 시조에서 FSTL이 모음으로 끝난다는 것을 알 수 있다. 이 점에서는 김정화의 주장은 근거가 있다.

통사구조에서는 어떠한가? FSTL이 통사적으로 독립되어 있지 않다면, 이것이 단일구로서 독립된 한 장을 차지한다는 이론은 근거가 없게 된다. 감탄사 또는 상투어가 쓰인 FSTL은 그 자체로 통사적으로 독립되었다고 볼 수 있다. 박을수의 시조대사전을 보면 처음 200수 중 62수가 통사적으로 독립된 FSTL을 갖고 있다. 이는 31%이며 황진이의 6 수 시조 중에서는 통사적으로 독립된 FSTL이 없다. 모든 것을 고려했을 때, 한 구 한 장, FSTL 자체가 독립된 한 개의 Line이라는 주장은 근거가 충분해 보이지 않는다.

여기서 언급해야 할 것이 하나 더 있다. 3장 6구의 구를 나누는 것은, 구의 앞뒤로 휴지(休止)가 기대되기 때문이다. 붙여서 읽을 거라면 굳이 구를 나눌 필요는 없다. SSTL이 지금까지 이해되어온 대로 하나의 구가 아니라, 두 개의 구로 되어 있다는 김정화의 주장에 동의하기는 어렵다. 그런 주장은 시조 리듬과 종장에서의 반전을 중시하지 않는 주장인 것으로 보인다. SSTL이 한번에 이어져서 읽히지 않고, 두번에 나뉘어서, 두 개의 segment로, 읽힌다면, 어떻게 되는가? 종장에서의 긴장감이나 반전이 없어지고 오직 segment의 밋밋하고 지루한 나열만 있게 된다. 종장에서의 반전은 SSTL이 다른 segment 보다 더 길지만 하나의 segment로 발음이 된다는 점에 있다. 따라서 이 주장에 따르면 종장에서의 반전이 없어져버린다.

예를 들어, 양사언의 시조에서 김정화의 주장대로 한다면, "사람이 // 제 아니 // 오르고 // 뫼만 높다 // 하더라" 하고 읽어야 한다는 말이 된다. 한국인의 시조감각이란 이 경우, "사람이 // 제 아니 오르고 // 뫼만 높다 // 하더라"로 읽어서, "제 아니 오르고"를 중간에 끊지 않고 읽는 데서 묘미를 느끼는 것이 아닐까? 김정화의 주장대로 한다면, 시조 구조상의 균형감은 약간 기대될 수 있을지 모르나 종장에서의 반전에서 오는 시조의 역동성은 기대하기 어렵게 된다. 이것이 김정화의 주장에 동의하기 어려운 이유다. 그러나 이 주장은 시사하는 바가 있는데, 그것은 시조에서의 FSTL, SSTL이 차지하는 특별한 위치다.

2. The nature of the syllable count cadence

한국어는 중국어처럼 성조어가 아니고 영어처럼 엑센트의 언어도 아니다. 한국어는 성조와 액센트가 달라진다 해서 뜻이 달라지지는 않는다. 따라서 한국인들은 음절수에 의한 리듬을 개발해냈다.

3. The meaning of the Fixed Form

정형시이긴 하지만 형식의 견고성은 일본의 하이쿠나 중국의 절구처럼 엄격하지는 않다. 3개의 Line으로 되어 있고, 각 Line은 4마디로, 각 마디는 평균 4음절로 이루어졌고, FSTL은 3음절이어야 하고, SSTL은 5음절 이상 8음절 이하여야 한다는 점 말고는 형식이 유연하다. 각 마디는 1~2 음절 차이로 위의 표준구조 보다 더 길어지거나 짧아질 수 있는데 어떤 경우는 3음절 차이가 나기도 한다. 특히 SSTL인 경우가 그렇다. 이런 유연성에서 시조는 불완전한 정형시라고 불리고 있다.

4. 6구냐 12구냐

(1) Basics

a. number of Lines

시조가 3개의 Line으로 이루어져 있다는 점은 의문의 여지가 없다. Line의 수는 4 이상이 될 수 없다. Line은 세 개가 되어야 한다. 단장시조, 양장시조도 가능하다. 이 두 가지 변이형은 적어도 현재까지는 실험적인 것이다. 아직까지는 시조의 형식으로 광범위하게 인정받고 있다고 보기 어렵다. 그러나 이 두 가지 변이형은 시조의 본질이나 정의에 대하여 뭔가 통찰을 주고 있다는 것은 확실하다. 이 책에는 반영호 시인의 단장시조가 실려 있다.

b. even number of segments in one Line

우선 시조의 어떤 Line도 3마디나 5마디가 될 수 없다는 것을 기억해야 할 것이다. 한 Line의 마디 수는 2 또는 4가 되어야만 한다. 이는 견고한 규칙으로서 몇 개의 Line으로 쓰여진 것이든 상관 없이 평시조에서는 지켜져야 하는 규칙이다.

c. same duration for each segment

한 시조에서, 각각의 마디가 차지하는 시간은, 같다. 각각의 마디(segment)가 발음되는 데는 같은 시간이 걸려야 한다. 이는 보다 많은 음절로 구성된 마디는 시간을 맞추기 위해서는 다소 빨리 발음되어야 함을 의미한다. 또한 각 마디끼리 음절수의 균형이 어느 정도 유지되어야 한다. 한 마디는 다른 마디 보다 지나치게 늘어날 수 없다. 한 마디가 차지하는 길이가 무제한이라면, 정형시라는 것도 리듬도 무의미해진다.

d. arbitrary Line break

Line을 끊어서 읽는 Line Break는 같은 시조의 같은 Line이라도 읽는 사람마다 다를 수 있다는 것이다. 끊어읽기는 자의적이긴 하지만, 마디 마다 같은 시간이 걸려야 하기 때문에 지나치게 자의적일 수는 없다.

(2) What's the difference?

6 마디 주의와 12 마디 주의가 어떻게 다른가? 6 마디라면 시조의 각 Line이 2 마디로 끊어서 읽을 수 있게 되어 있다면 충분하고 다시 더 끊어읽게 할 필요가 없다. 이 때는 정형시라는 형식이 다소 이완된다. 작가의 입장에서 볼 때는 더 자유로와지기 때문이다. 그러나 12 마디라면, 작가는 각 Line이 4 마디로 끊어 읽어질 수 있게끔 장치를 해야만 하고, 각 마디가 차지하는 시간도 대략 비슷해야 하므로 부담이 가중된다.

좀 더 가까이서 자세히 살펴보자. 장경렬은 '시조의 영역을 위한 하나의 시론(試論)- 현대비평과 이론 24호(2005년도 발표)'에서 다음과 같이 말하고 있다. [[(1)시조란 대체로 3장 6구에 43자의 글자로 이루어진 정형시가라는 데 이의를 제기할 사람은 아마도 없을 것이다(p 177). (2)우리 문단의 적지 않은 시조 시인들의 시조에 대한 인식이 3장 6구에 대략 43자의 음절로 이루어진 정형시라는 선에 머물러 있지는 않은가를 반성해보아야 할 것이다(p 182).]]

3장 6구 주장에 반대할 사람은 없겠지만 6구로 충분하다고 생각할지는 확실치 않다. 실제로 많은 사람들은 시조는 12구로 나뉘어질 수 있어야 한다고 믿는 듯 하다. 오히려 12구 주장이 대세인 것으로 보인다. 평시조에 국한해서 볼 때, 12 마디 주의가 널리 지지를 받고 있으며 많은 사람들이 6구로만 나뉘어지는 것으로는 충분치 못하고, 12구로도 나뉘어져야만 믿는다는 걸 알 수 있다. 고시조, 현대시조를 막론하고 6구로는 나뉘어지지만 12구로는 나뉘어질 수 없는 시조는 찾아보기가 어렵기 때문이다. 위 저자가 6구를 지지한다는 말이 12구를 배척하는 취지인지, 즉 하나의 시조가 6개의 구로 나뉘어지면 충분하고 12구로 나뉘어져야만 할 필요는 없다는 취지인지 아니면 12구로도 나뉘어져야만 한다고 믿지만, 굳이 12라는 말을 안 하고 3장 6구라고 했던 것인지는 분명하지 않다.

위 저자는 이색의 시조에 대한 자신의 영어번역을 제시하면서 6줄 배열은 시조의 6 마디 주의 구조에 충실하고자 하는 의도를 반영했다고 쓰고 있다.

In the valley of deep snows
    The clouds are cold and dreary;
Oh, lovely plum flowers,
    Where are you blooming now?
Standing alone at sunset,
    I am wondering where to go.

이제, 6 마디 주의와 12 마디 주의가 어떤 차이가 있는지 살펴보자. 장경렬이 번역한 시조는 다음과 같이 12 마디로 끊어읽을 수 있을 것이다:

In the valley // of deep snows
    The clouds are // cold and dreary;
Oh, lovely plum flowers,
    Where are you // blooming now?
Standing alone // at sunset,
    I am wondering // where to go.

세 번 째 줄, "Oh, lovely plum flowers"은 (A) "Oh, lovely // plum flowers" 또는 (B) "Oh, // lovely plum flowers"로 될 것이다. (A)에서는 끊어읽기에 규칙성이 부족하여 너무 자의적으로 보인다. 영어 원어민의 자연스러운 끊어읽기는 (B)가 될 것이다. (B)의 경우에는 "lovely plum flowers"가 "Oh"에 비해서 너무 길어졌다. 12 마디 주의에서 볼 때, 이 "Oh"는 단음절 마디가 된다.

여기서, 12 마디 주의일 경우 우리는 6 마디 주의에서는 나타타지 않는 다음과 같은 질문을 만나게 된다. "Ah!나 Oh! 같은 단음절 마디도 허용되는가?

단음절 마디는 매우 드물다. 박을수의 한국시조대사전을 보면 처음 200 수의 시조에서 단음절 마디는 나타나지 않는다. 임종찬은 "현대시조 탐색(2009년 출판)"이라는 책에서 "우리 시에 한 음절이 한 음보를 이루는 경우가 없다는 점에서"라고 언급하고 있다. 나는 단음절 마디는 허용되지 말아야 한다고 믿는다. 6구가 시조작자에게 더 자유를 준다는 것을 알 수 있다. 그렇지만 12구로 씌어진 시조는 리듬감이 더 좋게 느껴진다. 우리는 시조가 12구로 씌어야 한다고 믿기 때문에 엄밀하게 12구를 지키려고 노력했다.

5. FSTL, the first segment of the third Line

(1) The nature of FSTL

일부 고시조에서는 종장첫구로 상투어가 쓰였다: 두어라, 아희야, 차라리, 아마도, 어떻다, 진실로, 이렇게, 어디서, 그 중에, 아무리, 어즈버 등. 이들 상투어를 우리는 'universal phrases', 'set phrases' or 'regulated phrases' 등으로 부를 수 있다. 어떤 학자는 FSTL에 상투어가 주로 쓰였다는 주장을 하는 듯이 보인다. '시조의 외국어 번역에 관한 시론 - 시조의 감성 구조와 투어의 활용을 중심으로(2009년 발표)'에서 조태성은 "regulated words"라는 용어를 썼다. 그는 FSTL에서의 상투어 사용은 누구나 인정하는 것이며 시조를 시조답게 하는 필수불가결한 요소라고 주장하면서 다음과 같이 말하고 있다;

[[현대의 창작시조든 시조의 번역이든 간에 FSTL에는 상투어가 쓰여야 한다. 그렇지 않으면 독자들이 자기가 읽고 있는 것이 시조인지 아닌지 알기 어려울 수 있기 때문이다. 상투어가 FSTL에 쓰이지 않으면 시조다움은 줄어든다.]]

위 시론의 저자가 주장하듯이 FSTL에 주로 상투어나 감탄사가 쓰였는지 살펴본다. 문제는 그런 상투어, 감탄사가 압도적이었는가 하는 것이다. 그렇지는 않았던 것으로 보인다. 박을수 시조사전을 보면 처음 200 수 중에서 62 수만이 FSTL에서 상투어를 사용했다. 이 사실은 FSTL의 본질이 상투어, 감탄사라는 주장에 강한 의문을 제기하고 있다. 이 시론이 말하는 것은 극단적이다. 여기에 더하여 시론은 FSTL이 3음절로 고정되어야 한다고 주장한다.

현대시조는 어떤가? 현대시조는 그런 상투어를 FSTL에 사용하지 않는다. 그렇지만 저자가 제기하는 주장은 아무 근거가 없는 것은 아니다. 시조가 불완전한 정형시라면 FSTL에 대한 그런 제한은 장점이 있을 수 있다. 시론에서 언급되었듯이 FSTL에 상투어가 쓰이면 독자들은 자기가 읽는 것이 시조라는 것을 더 쉽게 알 수 있는 잇점도 있다고 볼 수 있다.

그 점을 고려한다 해도, 시조를 그런 상투어에 묶어놓으면 시조를 위축시키고 지나친 부담을 줄 수 있다. 자연스러운 흐름을 막고 폭발적인 시상(詩想)을 위축시킬 수 있다. 시조는 시조시인에 족쇄로 작용하여 시조를 무기력하게 할 수 있다. 두 가지 선택이 가능한데 왜 하나를 버리는가? 시론에서 제기하는 문제점은 다른 방법으로 해결할 수 있다. 또한 현대시조는 FSTL에서 상투어를 쓰지 않는다는 점도 고려해야 한다. 우리 나름대로의 해결방법은 Display Format에서 제시될 것이다.

(2) The three-syllable structure of FSTL

현대시조에서 정상급 시조작가일 뿐만 아니라 여동생 이영도 시조시인과 함께 현대시조의 새로운 경지를 개척한 것으로 평가받는 이호우는 '할아버지'라고 쓸 곳에서 '할버지'라고 썼다. 할아버지를 할버지라 하는 것은 아주 어린 아이나 쓸 만한 말일 것이다. 이 예는 FSTL가 얼마나 중요하게 여겨지고 있는가를 보여주고 있다.

그러나 텍스트 시조에서든 가곡창에서든 FSTL이 3음절이어야 하는 뚜렷한 이유가 있어보이지는 않는다. FSTL이 3음절이어야 한다는 전통이 왜 생겼는가 하는 이유를 찾을 수 없었음을 인정한다. 전통이었으리라 추정할 뿐이다. 조동일 교수가 힌트를 주고 있다. 그의 책에서 종장에서의 감탄사는 신라시대의 향가에도 있었던 전통이라고 쓰고 있다. 언어학적으로는 한국어에서 감탄사는 대개 3음절로 되어 있다.

박을수 시조대사전의 400 수 중에서 17 개만이 3 음절이 아닌 형식으로 되어 있다. 영어시조에서는 어떤가? FSTL은 역시 3음절이어야 하는가? 영어시조에서도 3음절로 고정하면 얻는 것 보다는 잃는 것이 더 많다고 본다. 한국어와 달리 영어는 감탄사가 주로 3음절이 되는 것이 아니기 때문이다. 그러므로 영어시조에서는 이런 구속이 더 느슨해져야 한다. 그러나 이것이 FSTL이 차지하는 특별한 위치가 영어시조에서는 필요하지 않다거나 FSTL이 무제한으로 길게 늘어질 있다는 걸 의미하지는 않는다. 더 자세한 내용은 Display Format에서 다뤄질 것이다.

6. The reversal in the last Line

주목할 만한 것이, 구조에서는 가장 중요할 수도 있는 것이, 종장에서의 twist and turn이다. 이는 정통적이며 전통적인 것이다. 이런 반전은 의미에서만 있는 것이 아니라 형식에서도 있다. SSTL은 이런 반전을 위해서 길어진다. 독자들에게 분위기가 달라지고 있음을 알려주고, 다가오는 클라이막스와 종료를 암시한다. 막힘 없는 유연한 흐름이 목적지에 다와가자, 걸음을 재촉하여 할 말을 다 하고는 차차 가늘어져서 사라진다.

위에서 언급하였듯이 조동일은 광의의 시조와 협의의 시조를 FSTL과 SSTL에서의 음절수로 구분한다. "FSTL은 기준음절수 미달인 2자나 3자이고, SSTL은 기준음절수 초과인 5자나 6자인 것은 협의의 시조이다"라고 적고 있다. 이걸 관점을 달리 해서 보면, 종장에서 걸음을 재촉하는 점이 있는가 없는가로 구분하고 있음을 알 수 있다. 각 마디를 읽는 시간은 똑 같은 것으로 고정되어 있기 때문에, 음절수 늘어나면 시간을 맞추기 위해서 빨리 읽어야 할 것이기 때문이다. 적어도 형식에 있어서의 이런 반전은 시조에서 필수적인 것이다. 그래서 조동일은 윤선도의 어부사시사를 협의의 시조가 아닌 광의의 시조로 분류한다. 종장에서의 형식상의 반전이 없기 때문이다.

그러나 종장의 중요성을 감안하더라도 SSTL은 그 부여받은 임무를 다하기에는 버거워 보인다. 정말로 반전을 하려고 했다면 3+4에서 3+5로의 변화의 정도는 너무 미약한 것이다. 변화 그리고 차이는 별로 크게 느껴지지 않는다. 이 점에서 본다면, 불완전한 장치라 볼 수 있다. 이런 불완전성은 시조가 노래로 출발했다는 데서 온다고 볼 수 있다. 음악 반주에 맞춘 공연에서는 그 차이가 두드러졌었을 수 있다. SSTL이 시각적으로 그리 두드러지지 않는다는 점을 고려해볼 때, 종장에서의 반전이 그렇게 강조되고 있는 현실은 이해하기 어려운 점이 있다. 3+4에서 3+5로의 전환이 그렇게 큰 변화인가? 현대시조는 음절수가 좀 더 자유롭기 때문에 긴 음절이 빈번히 사용되고 있고 따라서 SSTL에서의 반전은 더욱 덜 두드러지게 된다.

대조와 차이가 충분히 느껴지지 않는다면 시조는 다소 지루해진다. 3 줄짜리 자유시가 되어버릴 수가 있다. 그러므로 오늘의 시조는 그 어머니인 음악으로서의 시조가 소멸된 후, 오래된 전통의 단순반복에 불과하다고 말할 수도 있을 지 모른다. 전통에 갇힌 고아. 시조는 과거에 음악의 도움을 받았으나 이제는 밖으로 내몰려, 자신을 방어할 변변한 것도 없이, 호올로 서 있다. 오늘날 시조가 별로 인기가 없는 것이 놀라운 일이 아니다. 사람들은 시조를 별로 읽지 않는다. 3+4 음절의 반복은 특별히 대단히 잘 쓰이지 않는다면, 상투적이고 단조로운 느낌을 불러오기 쉽다. 사람들은 서구의 자유시 영향을 받아서 탄생한 자유시를 더 좋아한다.

종장에서의 특별한 뭔가가 필요하다. 이 특별하다는 것이 자동적으로 '3+5 음절'이 되는 것은 아니다. 어쩌면 우리가 시조를 더 정교한 형식으로 발전시켜야 할 때가 되었는지도 모른다. 음악의 도움 없이도 톤의 변화를 더 두드러지게 하려면, SSTL은 훨씬 더 길어져야 한다. 차이와 불균형이 확실하게 읽히고 들리고 느껴지게끔. FSTL이 현재의 3음절을 초과해서 더 길어진다면, 예를 들어, 5음절 정도로 길어진다면, SSTL도 그 비율만큼 더 길어져야 한다. 대략 10~12 음절 정도?

이런 뚜렷한 톤의 변화는 시조의 정체성을 더 확실한 바탕 위에 세운다는 점 외에 시조를 더 재미있게 할 것이다. 시가로서의 시조의 어머니인 음악이 사라졌다는 것을 잊지 말아야 하는 건지도 모른다. 음악이 사라졌다 함이 시조창, 가곡창이 더 이상 공연되지 않는 다는 말이 아니라, 시조가 시조 자체로 독립되어서 창작되고 있지, 시조창, 가곡창을 위한 가사로 창작되고 있는 것이 아니라는 뜻이다. 음악이 차지했던 장소는 이제 비어 있어서 뭔가로 채워져야 한다. 지금까지는 그 장소는 완전히 채워지지 않고 있다.

3+4에서 3+5로의 변화는 충분치 못하다. SSTL은 자신의 존재를 부각시키기 위해서는 지금 보다 현저히 더 길어져야 한다. 우리는 SSTL의 이런 특별한 성질 즉 다른 segment 보다 훨씬 더 길고 그렇기 때문에 발음할 때는 같은 시간 내에 끝내기 위해서 약간 서둘러서 발음된다는 걸 번역에 반영하려고 했다.

7. Patterned Phrase as the third Line

FSTL에서의 상투어를 떠나서 보더라도, 많은 경우에 종장 전체가 상투어로 되어 있기도 했다. 이임수는 "시조 종장의 관용화 현상에 대한 검증, 1992년 발표"에서 검증 결과를 발표했다. 전체 고시조의 1/7 정도인 682 수의 시조에서 13%인 89 수가 종장 전체가 상투어였다. 그렇다면 10 % 이상의 고시조에서 종장 자체가 상투어였다는 말이 된다.

8. Last line is the conclusion of Shijo

종장은 다른 관점에서 보면, 언제나 결론을 제시하고 있다고 볼 수 있다. 형식과 의미에서의 반전은 결국 시조의 결론이 된다. 작가의 명확한 결론이 없는 좋은 시조는 드물다. 그 이유는 고려시대부터 등장하기 시작한 신진사대부가 시조를 시작했기 때문일 수 있다. 신진사대부는 정치적, 이데올로기적인 이유 때문에 시조를 쓴 것으로 보인다. 그래서 결론이 필요했다. 정치적인 이유라면 왕의 사랑을 요구하거나 세상에 대한 불만 표출, 유교적인 이데올로기를 표명하기 위한 것이었다.

9. Easy Flow

시조가 음악에 맞춰서 노래하기 위하여 쓰여졌으므로 자연스러운 흐름이 필수였다. 현대시조도 노래를 의식하지 않지만 이런 전통을 잘 반영하고 있다. 좋은 시조는 흐름이 부드럽다. 그래서 시조는 어렵게 쓰이지 않고, 무겁지 않고, 지나치게 감추려 하지 않으며, 고도로 정교한 테크닉을 구사하지 않는다. 자연스러운 흐름을 위해서 마침표나 세미콜론 등의 구두점은 꼭 필요한 경우가 아니라면 잘 쓰이지 않는다.

10. Enjambment

양다리 걸치기 기법(enjambmemt)이란 한 line의 마지막 부분이 다음 line의 일부로 기능하는 수법이다. T.S. Eliot는 그의 시, '황무지'의 도입부에서 이 수법을 사용했다:

사월은 가장 잔인한 달
죽은 대지에서 라일락을 키워내고
기억과 욕망을 뒤섞고
봄비로 잠이 덜 깬 뿌리를 흔들어 깨운다.
겨울은 따뜻했다.
잊어버리게 하는 눈으로 대지를 덮고
어린 것에게 마른 구근을 먹였다.

주제에 집중하기 위해서 "enjambment"를 한 Line의 마지막 마디가 다음 Line의 일부로 기능하는 테크닉이라고 정의하자. Line 기준이 아닌 line 기준의 enjambment는 이 책에서, 일곱줄 배열을 채택했기 때문에, 많이 등장한다. Line 기준 enjambment는 고시조에서 드물게 나타난다. 분명하고 뛰어난 예는 193면에 나와 있는 "어져, 내 일이야"로 시작하는 황진이의 시조에서 "제 구태야"이다. 그 테크닉은 영어로 옮겨지면서 번역에 반영되지 못했다.

11. Sophisticated Enjambment

"세련된 enjambment 기법"이라고 불러도 좋을 만한 기법이 있을 수 있다. enjambment가 단순한 물리적 배열의 문제라면, 이 테크닉은 더 발달한 수법이다. 한 마디가 앞의 마디에 연결되어 해석될 수도 있고, 다음 마디에 연결되어 해석될 수도 있는데, 그 두 가지가 다 말이 되고, 그래서 더 다양한 뜻을 머금게 되는 경우를 말한다.

"제 구태야"가 중장의 일부로 해석되어서, "제 구태여 갔겠는가?"로 이해될 수도 있고, 종장의 일부로 해석되어서, "나 구태야 보내고 그리는"으로 이해될 수도 있다. 실제로는 이 두 가지를 다 뜻하게끔 의도되었을 수가 있다. 이는 놀라운 기법이다. 작자는 남자를 떠나보내려고 하지 않았으나 "구태여" 그렇게 해버린 셈이 되었고, 남자 역시 떠나려 하지 않았으나 어떤 이유에선지 "구태여" 여자를 떠난 셈이 되었다. 엄격한 정형의 틀 안에서, 작자는 이 복잡한 상황과 복잡한 두 사람의 마음을 고도로 세련된 enjambment 기법을 사용하여 우리에게 당시 상황을 생생하게 그림을 그려서 전달해주고 있다. 16세기에 이런 고도의 테크닉을 구사했던 시조 작가가 있었다는 사실은 진실로 놀랍지 아니한가?

이 책에도 다른 시조의 영어번역에서 그 기법이 나온다. 178 페이지에 나오는 시조 번역이다.

> The two Buddha, naked and starved
> face each other, on the road
> rain or wind, snow or frost
> they will only have to suffer.
> They never know,
> human separation,
> I do envy those two Buddha.

"rain or wind, snow or frost"은 앞의 두 행에 이어서 이해될 경우에는, "비 오든 바람 불든, 눈이 오든 서리 맞든"이란 뜻이 되고, 다음 행에 붙여서 이해될 경우에는, "비와 바람과 눈과 서리를 견뎌야만 한다, 피할 도리가 없다"는 뜻이 된다. 그 두 가지 뜻을 모두 내포하는 것으로 이해할 수도 있다.

12. Enjambment in terms of verses

종장은 항상 시조 전체의 결론에 해당하여 시조를 맺어야 하는가? 현대의 연시조는 종장이 시조를 끝맺지 않고 다음 연에 의미적으로, 통사적으로 연결되어 마치 다음 연의 초장으로 기능하는 것을 허용하는 경우가 많다. 이는 연과 연 사이의 양다리 걸치기 수법이라고 부를 수 있을 것이다.

연과 연 사이의 양다리 걸치기도 허용이 되는가? 많은 시조대회 수상작들이 그렇게 쓰이고 있다. 보수적인 사람들은 반대한다. 그런 경우에는 시조가 3 장이 아니라는 것이다. 종장이 다음 연의 초장으로 기능하므로 단지 3장으로 배열이 되어있을 뿐이라는 것이다. 이게 허용이 되면 작가는 두 가지 선택의 여지가 있으므로 더 많은 자유를 누리게 된다. 그렇다면 시조의 3장 구조는 어느 정도의 중요성이 있는가? 필자는 보수적인 쪽에 서고 싶다. 종장은 결론이 되어야지 다음 연의 초장으로 기능할 수 없다.

Display Format

시조는 3 부분 또는 3 행으로 나뉘어진다. 그렇지 않으면 시조가 아니다. 양장, 단장시조도 가능하겠지만 여기서는 평시조를 다루고 있다. 시조의 세 부분은 '장(Line)'이라 한다. 대문자 'Line'은 시조의 '장'을 의미하기로 한다. 몇 줄로 시조를 배열하는가도 논란의 대상이다. 고시조는 음악반주를 고려하여 5 부분으로 배열되었다고 한다. 물론 많은 시조가 띄어쓰기도 없이 쓰여졌는데 현대 한국어는 그런 식으로 쓰이지 않는다. 그러나 가곡창을 위한 배려에서 시조는 5 부분으로 나뉘어서 배열되었다고 믿어지고 있다.

가곡창을 위하여 시조가 5 줄로 배열되었다 하는 주장에 대하여 필자는 의구심을 갖고 있다. 실제로 가곡창을 들어본다면, 두 부분으로 되어 있다고 느낄 것이다. 간주 이전과 간주 이후. 5 줄 배열은 우연일 수 있다. 필수가 아니라. 즉, 그런 5 줄 배열은 당시에 만연하던 방식이 아니라, 한 두 권의 책에서 그렇게 배열되었었다는 정도 이상의 의미가 없는 것이 아닐까 하는 것이다. 그 근거는 5줄 배열 주장자들이 근거로 드는 것이 조선시대 안민영의 금옥총부 이외에 다른 근거를 제시하지 못한다는 것이다.

오늘날은 배열형식도 주목의 대상이 되고 있다. 결론부터 말하면, 배열을 어떻게 하는가는 상관할 필요가 없다는 것이다. 그건 작가가 알아서 할 일이다. 그러나 어떤 학자들은 다른 견해를 주장한다. 한국문학의 전도사로 불리는 Kevin O'Rourke은 "5줄 영어 포맷은 가곡창의 5 장 구조와 대체로 일치한다"라고 주장한다.

조태성은 '시조의 외국어 번역에 관한 시론 - 시조의 감성 구조와 투어의 활용을 중심으로'에서 조선시대에 쓰여진 안민영의 금옥총부에 "모든 시조들이 가곡창을 의식해서 5줄로 배열되었다"라는 말이 나온다는 주장을 인용하고 있다. 그러면서 5줄 배열은 시조를 영어로 번역할 때도 시조의 독특한 형식적 특징을 드러내기 위해서 따라야 한다고 역설한다.

다섯줄 배열은 처음 두 줄이 시조의 초장에 해당하고, 셋째 줄은 시조의 중장에 해당하고, 넷째줄은 FSTL이고, 마지막 줄은 그 다음 부분 전체가 된다. 이 5줄 배열이 더 보기 좋은가? 좋다고 동의하기는 어렵다. 5줄 배열이 가곡창을 위해서 개발된 것이라면 이런 의문이 떠오른다. 이제 시조가 음악에서 독립했는데 왜 다시 음악으로 돌아간단 말인가? 그건 후진하는 셈이 아닌가? 시조는 음악의 종속품이 아니다. 과거엔 어땠을 지 몰라도. 시조는 이제 독립한 자격을 갖추고 독립해있다. 그렇다면 왜 시조를 과거의 것에 맞춰서 결정해야 하는가?

Richard Rutt과 김제현 교수, 그리고 외무부 장관이었던 변영태는 1948년도에 출간된 'SONGS FROM KOREA'에서 6줄로 배열했다. 6줄 배열형식은 시조의 영어번역에서 정형으로 자리잡은 듯 하다.

Kevin O'Rourke은, "5줄 배열에도 문제가 좀 있다. 4번 째 줄이 특히 그렇다. 대개 의미론적으로 독립되어 있지 않기 때문이다. 음악적인 면에 대한 고려와 3음절로 잘려야 한다는 문학적인 텍스트 사이에서 타협을 할 수밖에 없었다"라고 그의 책에서 적고 있다.

조태성은 위에서 언급된 논문에서 다음과 같이 주장하고 있다: [[FSTL은 순수하게 감탄사적인 기능을 하거나 통사론적으로 의미 있는 기능을 수행한다. 전자의 경우에는 영어번역에서 문제가 없다. 감탄이 내용이므로 통사론적으로 독립되어 있기 때문이다. 그러나 후자의 경우에는 딜레머가 발생한다. 원 시조가 통사적으로 의미 있는 것을 쓴 것을 감탄사적인 상투어로 바꿔서 번역하기가 곤란해지는 문제가 생긴다. (이 책 편집자의 주석: 원 시조의 의미를 번역자가 바꿔버리는 셈이 되기 때문이라는 취지로 보임)]]

분명히 FSTL을 독립된 줄에 배열하는 것은 보기도 좋고, 재미도 있다. 적어도 전체 시조에서 FSTL이 차지하는 위상을 잘 반영한다. FSTL의 이런 특별한 위상이 없이는, 그리고 SSTL에서의 반전이 없다면 다른 종류의 운문과 시조가 어떻게 구분될 수 있는가? 3줄로 쓰인 자유시에 음절수 제한이 더해진 것과 크게 다른가?

FSTL이 독립된 줄에 배열되면 독자 또는 낭송자는 FSTL 직후에 잠시, 다른 segment 사이의 휴지 보다는 더 긴 휴지(休止)를 취할 것이고, 청중은 다음에 뭐가 나올지 기대하게 될 것이다. 이 휴지는 형식에서 그리고 낭송에서 시조다움을, 시조만의 형식을 보여줄 것이다. FSTL이 독립된 줄을 차지하려면 통사에서 그리고 의미에서 독립성을 갖춰야 한다. 그러나 100% 그래야할 필요는 없다. 예를 들어, “I'd rather”, “What can I”, “Whoever else”, “Let it be”, “What more is”, “Who would not” 등도 좋은 FSTL이 될 수 있다.

Conclusion of Display Format

우리는 7줄 배열을 채택했다. FSTL은 너무 중요해서 이것을 시조의 정수라고 해도 과장이 결코 아니다. 이 점에서 5 줄 배열 주장도 근거가 충분하다. 6줄 배열도 동의할 만 하다.

FSTL을 따로 떼어내서 한 줄에 배열하여, 7줄로 배열하면 작가와 번역자에게 부담이 가중된다. FSTL을 따로 배열하는 취지가 살아나야 하기 때문이다. 다음 줄과 독립되기도 해야 하고, 동시에 연결되기도 해야 한다. 그렇지 않으면 독립된 배열은 무의미한 일이 되어버린다. 그래서 독립성과 종속성을 동시에 요구한다. 한국어 시조도 이런 부담은 지지 않는다. FSTL을 따로 배열하지 않는 것이다. 그렇다면, 영어시조는 한국어 시조 보다 더 큰 제약하에 있게 된다. 그러나 영어시조는 FSTL이 3 음절이어야 한다는 한국어 시조의 제한이 없으므로 이걸 모두 감안하면 균형이 유지된다.

Grammar vs Cadence

이 책을 쓰면서 영어문법이 대두하였다. 리듬과 음보율은 시조의 생명이라서 이게 없으면 시조가 안 된다. 그렇지만 시조는 언어로 쓰인 것이고, 언어란 문법이 없으면 존재하지 않는다. 따라서 문법과 시조의 음보율이 충돌한다. 위에서 보았듯이 유명한 시조시인 이호우는 4음절 단어인 할아버지를 음보율을 고려하여 3음절 할버지로 썼다. 우리도 이런 문제에 부닥쳤다.

예를 들면 우리는 다음과 같이 썼다:

(A) You tell me what <u>was love</u> like.
(B) Don't be looking only <u>your steps</u>.

그렇지만 문법에 맞게 한다면 이렇게 되어야 할 것이다:

(A) You tell me what <u>love was</u> like.
(B) Don't be looking only <u>at your steps.</u>

문법에 맞는 표현이 리듬감이 부족하므로 우리는 덜 문법적인 채택할 수밖에 없었다. 그러나 덜 문법적인 표현은 이 책에서 매우 드물게 나타난다.

Rhyming

한국 시조는 고시조든 현대시조든 각운, 두운 등의 운율을 맞추지 않는다. 한국시조는 음수율을 맞춘다고 말할 수 있다. 영어 시는 운율을 강조하는 듯 하다. 영어와 달리 한국어는 비교적 운율저항적이라고 볼 수 있다. 시조와 가사가 한국어에서 등장한 이유들 중의 하나에 해당한다.

영어시조를 쓰거나 영어시조로 번역할 때, 운율이 문제가 된다. "자연스럽게"가 해답이라고 생각한다. 운율을 맞추는 것은 그렇게 맞췄을 때 더 아름답게 들려야만 의미가 있다. 영어는 한국어 보다 좀 더 운율친화적인 듯이 보이므로, 영어시조에서 굳이 운율을 배격할 필요는 없을 것이다. 영어시조에서 운율은 선택사항이 될 수 있을 것이다. 수주 변영로의 친형인 변영태는 1948년도에 운율을 맞춘 시조의 영어번역집을 "Songs From Korea"라는 제목으로 출판했었다. 우리 책에는 일부 시조가, 시조 한 수 전체에 걸쳐서, 또는 그 일부에 걸쳐서 운율이 맞춰져 있지만, 많지는 않다.

Arrangement in one Shijo

위에서 보았듯이 배열형식은 작가의 취향에 달려 있지만, 우리는 7줄 배열을 강력히 주장하고, FSTL은 독립되게끔 배열해야 한다고 본다. 시조의 줄 배열 다음에는 정렬을 고려할 만 하다. 이 책에서 보이는 정렬을 택하기는 했지만 다양한 정렬이 가능할 것이다. 이 책에서 현대시조는 원 시조의 배열을 대부분의 경우에 따랐다.

Afterword

필자가 전문학자가 아니기 때문에 위에서 언급된 저자들이 쓴 것을 전부 다 읽어본 것이 아니라는 점과 그렇기 때문에 여기에 인용된 의견들이 정확한 그 저자들의 의견과는 다를 수 있음을 분명히 하고자 한다.

후 기

김온승

얼마 전 설레는 마음으로 이 책의 초본을 받았다. 지금까지 책 출판에 참여해 본 적이 없는 나로서는 뿌듯한 느낌이 앞서야 했었지만 더 잘하지 못한 아쉬움이 컸다. 하지만 영어에 대한 남다른 관심을 가진 나에게 이 책 발행에 동참할 기회를 얻은 것은 커다란 행운이며 더구나 학교 친구들과 함께 색다른 경험을 할 수 있어서 뜻이 깊다.

이 책은 외국인들에게 시조를 알리기 위해 쓰여졌다. 종전에도 시조를 영어로 번역하려는 시도가 없었던 것은 아니다. 하지만 이때까지의 책들이 내용을 번역하는 데에 초점을 둔 데 비해 이 책은 시조의 형태를 유지하려고 했다는 점에서 뚜렷한 차이를 보여주고 있다. 시조는 초장, 중장, 종장으로 구성되어 있으며, 종장의 첫 음절은 3음보여야 하는 규칙을 가지고 있고 그 형태적 미와 내용이 결합했을 때 비로소 그 고유하고 독특한 맛을 제대로 감상할 수 있다. 시조 번역이 유난히 어려웠던 것도 바로 이 이유에서다. 간결성과 시조의 형태를 모두 고려해야 했고 시인만큼 단어 선택에도 어려움을 겪었다. 또한 고유명사가 나올 경우 음절이 너무 길어져 곤란했던 적도 많았다.

이런 어려움은 우리 모두의 문제였지만 다른 친구들은 이를 멋지게 해결했다. 실제로 이번 경험에서 가장 인상 깊었던 것은 친구들의 시조였다. 까다로운 조건들도 충족시켰을 뿐만 아니라 간결하며 시적인 표현도 멋지다. 이 활동은 본래의 취지대로 학생들 중심이었기 때문에 지도 선생님께서는 문법사항이나 단어의 적절성 정도만 지적해 주시고 나머지는 우리가 스스로 수정해 나갈 수 있게 이끌어 주셨다. 따라서 이 책의 번역시들은 우리 모두의 끊임

없는 교정과정을 거친 새로운 작품이라고 감히 말 할 수 있다.

우리 젊은 세대는 옛 것보다 새 것을 선호하는 경향이 짙다. 나도 예외는 아니어서 우리 선조들이 물려 준 자랑스런 문화유산을 잘 알고 지키고 발전시켜 나가는 일을 소홀히 해 왔다. 이 작업을 함께 수행해 가면서 때론 힘들고 포기하고 싶은 때도 많았지만 조상들의 아름다운 문학적 향기를 조금은 맛 볼 수 있어서 기뻤고 우리 선조들에 대한 후손으로서의 자부심을 느낄 수 있어서 값진 경험이 되었다. 또한 앞으로 영문학을 전공하고자 하는 나에게는 새로운 길을 제시해 준 고마운 기회가 되었다.

이 책이 나오기까지 많은 노력뿐만 아니라 세심한 배려가 필요했다. 현대시조를 싣기 위한 저작권 문제와 한글 발음을 고려한 표기 문제도 있었고 외국인의 의견을 듣기 위해 지인의 도움을 받기도 했다. 지도 선생님께서는 보다 나은 시조의 이해를 위해 작가의 환경과 배경 일화도 살펴보도록 권유하셨고 이를 통해 원저자와 동일한 환경과 입장에서 보다 나은 번역을 할 수 있게 되었다.

고마워해야 할 분이 너무 많다. 우선 친구들과 선생님, 부모님들께 감사 드린다. 특히 긴 시간 동안 가장 큰 고생을 하고 변함없는 열정을 보여주신 지도 선생님께 진심으로 감사 드린다. 미흡한 영어실력에 도움이 되었던 한컴사전도 공이 크다. 끝으로 이 책을 읽은 외국인들이 먼 동방의 나라 한국의 전통 있고 격조 높은 문학의 향기를 깊이 음미하게 되고 자랑스런 나의 조국 대한민국을 더 깊이 알아가는 기회가 되기를 간절히 소망한다.

후 기

박재우

시조를 전혀 알지 못했을 때였다. 선생님의 제안을 받고는 내가 책을 쓴다는 그 자체로 좋아 시작한 듯싶다. 2년 동안 이어진 작업이었지만 나에게 부담이 되었다고 생각하지는 않는다. 시조를 번역하는 과정자체가 진심으로 즐거웠고 내가 번역한 시들이 선생님의 채택목록에 하나하나 올라갈 때마다 나름대로의 성취감이 있었다. 뜻이 있는 선생님, 그리고 영민한 고등학교 친구들과 함께 작업하는 과정에서 많은 것을 얻을 수 있었다.

첫째로, 시조 번역 작업을 통해 시의 맛을 느낄 수 있었다. 요즘 학생들은 영화나 소설은 많이 보지만 시에는 크게 관심이 없는 것 같다. 영화관엘 가고 소설책을 사서 보지만 시집을 사지는 않는다. 아마 시를 영화나 소설과 같은 문화 생활의 한 갈래로 보기보다는 문학 시간에 배우는 교과과정쯤으로 생각하는 듯하다. 나 또한 같았다. 그러나 번역 작업을 하며 우리의 시조를 소리 내어 읽어보고, 동시에 그 의미를 곱씹어보고 말하는 이의 감정을 함께 느끼려 하는 순간, 처음으로 내 마음에 그 은은한 아름다움이 들어왔다.

거기에 그치지 않고, 우리말의 시조를 영어로 바꾸어 하나의 영시로 탄생시키고, 직접 만든 그 결과물을 다시 소리 내어 리듬을 타며 읽어볼 때는 특별한 짜릿함을 느낄 수 있었다. 바로 이 짜릿함이 오랜 작업을 즐길 수 있는 원동력이 되었다.

내가 가장 좋아하는 시조는 이조년의 시조다.

> Moon breaks white on pear blossoms
> and milky-way reaches into midnight.
> The night bird, how could it know
> the feels of coming spring hidden in a branch?
> I could not,
> sleep a wink, even a wink tonight,
> as if it were an illness, the sensitivity to me.

시조의 가장 큰 매력은 아마 그 리듬감에 있을 것이다. 이 시를 처음 번역하고 다시 운율에 맞추어 읽어봤을 때 처음으로 시조의 아름다움을 발견할 수 있었다. 시의 아름다운 내용이 시조의 운율과 결합되어 독특한 미가 느껴진다. 특히 종장의 3-5-4-3 리듬이 나에게는 너무 매력적이었다. 이 시를 번역한 후로 작업에 더욱 탄력이 붙었다. 즐길 수 있게 된 것이다. 처음 번역한 그대로 책에 실리지는 못했는데 아래가 바로 첫 번째 번역이다.

> Moon breaks / white on pear
> Milk's dropped / in mid air
> How could an / owl know
> Feeling of / coming spring
> I could not
> Sleep a wink tonight
> For the tenderness / like a fever

이조년의 시는 원본의 내용이 좋아 마음에 든 반면, 아래의 반영호의 <갈대>라는 한 줄짜리 시는 나의 번역본 중 가장 잘 되었다고 생각하는 시이다.

> 꽃인 듯
> 꽃도 아닌 꽃을
> 꽃처럼 피웠구나
>
> Like a flower,
> you blossomed a flower
> which isn't a flower shaped like a flower.

이것은 초역 그대로 책에 실릴 수 있었다. 한 줄밖에 안되지만 보통의 평시조보다 훨씬 어려웠던 것 같다. 꽃이란 단어가 각 음보의 두운으로 네 번 나오는 것이 이 시의 가장 중요한 부분이라 생각하고 네 번의 음보 끝에 모두 flower를 넣어 각운을 맞추었다. 번역을 완성하고 아주 기뻤던 기억이 난다.

번역작업은 영어공부에도 큰 도움이 되었다. 딱딱한 영어가 아니라 살아있는 영어 말이다. 영어에 대한 지식이라기보다는 감각을 배웠다고 말하고 싶다. 직접 시의 운율을 맞추기 위해 각 행을 늘였다 줄였다 하는 과정에서 문장 내에서의 생략의 허용범위를 느낄 수 있는 직감이 생겼다. 생략이라는 것은 시의 간결성을 위해 필수적인 요소다. 그러나 적절하게 생략하는 것은 쉬운 일이 아니다. 정확한 문법 지식뿐 아니라 영어 자체에 대한 감각이 필요하기 때문이다. 최대한 줄이되 의미를 전달하는 데에는 문제가 없어야 가장 좋은 문장이 된다. 고급의 단계로 들어갔을 때, 나는 생략을 잘하는 사람이 영어를 잘하는 사람이라고 생각한다. 그리고 영어로 시를 쓰는 일은 간결한 표현과 생략에 능숙해지는 최고의 방법이다. 나는 이 작업을 통해 좋은 영어 문장을 쓸 수 있는 힘을 얻었다고 생각한다.

아래는 내가 김소월의 <고락>을 번역하는 중 한 부분에 멈춰 한참 고민하고 있을 때 선생님이 주신 아이디어로 번역한 부분이다.

> Sweet or sour's in the mouth
> 먹이의 달고 씁은 입에 달리고
>
> Success or failure's in the mind
> 영욕의 苦와 樂도 맘에 달렸소

'A depend on B'보다 훨씬 좋은 표현이다. 'A be in B', 'A가 B에 달렸다'를 표현하는 말 중 가장 간결하고 좋은 표현이 아닌가 생각이 든다. 또한 'Whether it's sweet or sour', 'Whether it's success or failure'를 'Whether it's'를 생략해서 표현하니 이보다 더 간결할 수 없다. '먹이의 달고 씁은 입에 달렸다'를 'It depends on the mouth whether it's sweet or sour'로 표현하는 것과 'Sweet or sour's in the mouth'로 표현하는 것은 확실히 수준 차이가 난다.

또한 아래는 같은 시의 또 다른 부분이다.

> Don't be looking only your steps
> 기구한 발뿌리만 보지 말고서

Look at의 at을 생략해도 의미 파악에는 아무 문제가 없다. 틀린 표현이라고 말할 수도 있겠지만 내게는 간결해서 좋게만 느껴진다.

아래는 이영도의 <무제 1>이라는 시에 나오는 부분이다.

> Two of us with weary hearts
> 서로 야윈 가슴
>
> would only look out the window.
> 먼 창만 바라다가

'먼 창만 바라다가'라는 말에는 창 밖 멀리를 바라본다는 의미가 들어있다. 이를 그대로 번역하려 하니 길이가 계속 길어져 난감했다. 최대한 줄여도 'Look out of the window'정도였다. 그런데 out 뒤에 바로 the window를 넣어보니 괜찮아졌다. Out과 of는 항상 붙어 다녀야 하는 줄 알았는데 때론 of를 뺐을 때 간결하면서도 의미를 더 정확히 전달할 수 있다는 것을 알았다.

수많은 유의어 중 가장 적절한 단어를 찾는 과정에서는 여러 영단어들의 정확한 의미와 느낌을 알 수 있었다. 특히 시라는 것이 짧고 굵은 문장들로 이루어지기 때문에 단어 하나에 모든 심혈을 기울여야 했다. 짧으니 정확해야 한다는 뜻이다. 그리고 formal한 단어와 informal한 단어를 구별하면서 시에 필요한 informal한 단어를 많이 공부할 수 있었다. 영단어의 느낌에 대한 이해는 나의 영어 실력을 한층 올려주었다.

또한 내가 쓴 영어 문장이 실제로 원어민에게도 자연스럽게 느껴질까를 고심하고 거듭 수정하는 과정에서 원어민의 감각을 조금씩 배워갈 수 있었다. 같은 한국인끼리는 이해하지만 오히려 원어민은 이해하지 못할 때가 있는 걸 보고 놀랐다. 또한 내가 그런 문장을 얼마나 많이 쓰고 있었는가를 깨닫고는 더욱 놀랐다. 쉽게 콩글리쉬라고 표현할 수 있겠다. 콩글리쉬를 고치고 영어의 감각을 배울 수 있어 기뻤다. 전체적으로 시조 번역 작업은 내 영어 실력을 크게 끌어올려주었다고 느낀다.

영어 공부뿐 아니라 우리의 시조 문학 자체에 대해서도 깊은 공부를 할 수 있었는데, 특히 처음엔 서문 작성을 내가 맡아서 나름대로 도서관을 다니며 시조에 대해 능동적으로 공부해보는 기회도 가질 수 있었다. 그리고 번역하는 과정에서 학교에서 배우는 시조 거의 모두를 다루었기 때문에 고등학교 교과 과정 수준의 시조에는 큰 자신감이 붙었고 시험기간에도 오랫동안 붙잡고 공부할 필요가 없었던 듯 하다.

그러나 무엇보다도 이 작업을 통해 고등학교 공부를 넘어선 새로운 공부를 할 수 있었다는 점이 가장 기뻤다. 특히 처음에 서문 작성을 맡은 나에게 있어서는 더욱 그렇다. 책의 취지가 우리의 아름다운 시조를 영어로 올바르게 번역하여 세계에 알리고 나아가 현재 외국 작가들에 의해 창작되고 있는 영어시조의 기본원리와 규칙을 확립하는 하나의 틀을 만드는 데 있기 때문에, 서문은 이 책의 시작이자 가장 중요한 근간임에 틀림없다.

서문에서 영어시조의 정의를 내려야 하는데 그 과정이 생각보다 만만하지 않다. 새로운 정의를 내려야 하므로 논리력과 창의력이 동시에 필요한 어려운 작업이다. 원래의 우리시조의 정의와 기본원칙에 대해서 완벽히 이해하고 뚜렷한 자기주관을 가져야 함은 물론, 영어로 번역함에 있어 원 시조의 매력을 한껏 살리고 영어와 결합된 새로운 멋을 창조해내기 위한 몇 가지 아이디어를 착안해내야 했다. 선생님께서 제시하신 아이디어는 다음과 같다.

1) 초중종장의 '장'을 영어로는 대문자 'L'을 쓴 'Line'으로 쓴다.
2) 시조에서 중요한 의미를 가지는 종장 첫 번째와 두 번째 구를 각각 the first segment of the third Line, the second segment of the third Line을 줄여 FSTL, SSTL으로 쓴다.
3) 영어시조의 기본형식은 7줄로 한다. 초중종장을 각각 둘로 쪼개어 6줄로 하고 FSTL과 SSTL은 특별히 한 번 더 나누어 그 운율이 잘 드러나도록 한다.
4) 영어시조에서 FSTL은 3음절일 필요가 없다. 또한 감탄사 등과 같은 고정된 표현일 필요도 없다(근거는 책의 서문에 설명되어 있다).

서문을 보면 이 아이디어들과 함께 영어시조에 대한 명확한 정의가 제시되어 있는데 지금까지 나온 어떤 정의보다도 근거에 입각한 명쾌한 정의가 될 것이라 확신한다. 앞으로 세계에서 7줄로 된 영어시조가 널리 쓰여지기를 바란다. 비록 나는 서문작성을 해내지 못했지만 내가 이 일에 시도를 해보았다는 것만으로도 큰 보람을 느낀다.

소중한 우리 문학을 세계에 알리는 작업의 선두에 설 수 있어 기쁘다. 고등학생으로서 이 정도로 의미 있는 일을 할 수 있다는 것은 큰 축복일 것이다. 또한 작업하는 동안 실제로 학문이라는 것이 어떻게 이루어지는지 생생하게 느낄 수 있었다.

번역하는 동안 곁에서 지켜봐주신 어머니와 나를 믿어주신 선생님 그리고 함께 해준 친구들에게 감사하다는 말을 전하고 싶다.

시조는 항상 노래를 염두에 두고 읽어야 하는 특별한 시의 갈래이다. 세계인들에게 인기를 끌만한 충분한 매력을 지니고 있다. 오로지 우리의 관심과 노력에 달려있다고 본다. 후에 시조가 세계에서 큰 반향을 일으킬 날을 기대한다.

시조를 영어로 번역한다니

이정은

내가 처음 번역 팀에 들어가겠다고 결정했던 그 순간, 나는 노벨상에 대해 생각하고 있었다. 사람들은 한국 시인이 훌륭하긴 하지만 한국어의 묘미를 번역할 수 있는 번역가가 없어서 노벨상이든 뭐든 받지 못할 거라고 말했었다. 나는 번역판의 수준으로 문학의 수준을 결정짓는 것이 못내 못마땅했다. 그러나 국제 문단이 모두 한국어를 이해해 주기를 바라는 것은 무리였고 결국 중요한 것은 원작을 "살리는" 번역이라는 걸 금방 깨달았다.

모든 일을 끝내는 데에 거의 2년이 걸렸고 이제 나는 그것이 그만큼 가치 있는 일이었다고 말한다. 그러나 시조 한 줄 읽어 본 적 없는 15살짜리 여자애에겐 다른 일이었다. 처음에 나는 내가 한국 문학을 영어로 소개한다는 사실에 무척 고무되어 있었다. 그러나 기대가 크면 실망도 크다더니. 영어에 대해서는 사실 조금 걱정을 하기도 했지만 한국어는 내가 고려할 만한 것이 아니었다. 나는 내가 중세 국어를 "해독해야" 하는 줄은 꿈에도 몰랐다.

지금이야 중세 국어를 읽는 데 익숙해졌지만, 그 당시에 나는 꽤 좌절했었다. 내 모국어를 이해하기 위해 구글을 검색하는 것은 썩 유쾌하지만은 않은 일이었다. 내가 한 시조의 중심 개념을 이해하지 못할 때 마다 끝이 없던 나는 그만두고 싶었다. 하지만 그러질 못했다. 자원해서 시작한 건 나였고, 그건 곧 얼마나 힘든 일이든 간에 계속 해야만 한다는 것을 뜻했다. 자의 반 타의 반 계속하게 되었고 작업에 탄력이 붙기 시작했다.

번역은 내가 다소 조잡한 초고를 선생님께 보내면, 선생님이 내게 코멘트를 남기는 방식으로 진행되었다. 처음으로 10개의 시조를 보냈던 때가 기억난다. 말 그대로 최악이었다. 운문치곤 너무 길다. 너무 자의적이다. 상투적이다 등등. 나를 불평하게 만들었던 그 모든 코멘트들이 내 시조를 풍부하게 만들었고 나는 내가 해야 할 일이 해석이 아니라 참뜻을 고려하면서도 영미권 사람들에게 맞추어진 시를 재창작하는 것이라는 것을 깨닫게 되었다.

한편으로는 영어를 대하는 태도도 많이 바뀌었다. 이전엔 한국어와 영어의 비교를 통해 무언가를 표현하려고 했다면, 시간이 흐르면서 영어라는 언어의 느낌을 많이 체감하게 되었다. 시라는 장르의 특성 상 평소엔 생각조차 하지 못했을 생략도 과감히 시도하고, 문장 구조도 요리조리 바꾸어 보았다. 나중엔 시조에 관심이 있어서 온라인에 자신의 번역본을 올려놓은 외국인보다 더 나은 표현을 생각하려고 애쓰기도 했다.

다분히 문화적인 코드의 시를 번역하는 것은 어렵고, 내가 무언가 실수를 했을까 두렵기도 하다. 그러나 나는 우리의 훌륭한 문화적 소산을 세계에 스스로 소개한다는 것이 무척 영광되고, 행운이라고 생각한다. 세계인이 우리 시조를 감상하고, 더욱 발전시켜 시조를 다시 살려내는 날이 오기를 바란다.

시조 번역을 하고 나서

한재은

난해한 고전문학, 예전에는 그저 알 수 없는 언어로 느껴지던 그런 글들이었다. 고등학교 입학 숙제로 구운몽을 읽게 되었을 때가 생각이 난다. 구운몽을 읽으며 난해한 인물들의 고전적인 어투, 계속해서 바뀌는 사람을 지칭하는 말, 지나치게 늘여놓은 만연체 때문에 읽으면서 머리가 깨질 뻔 했던 기억이 아직도 생생하다. 맨 처음 시조를 번역하게 되었을 때도 마찬가지였다. 처음 접하게 되었을 때의 그 괴리감, 글로 설명할 수 없을 것 같다. 무슨 말인지 잘은 모르겠지만 이 난해한 글에 대해 막연한 호기심이 생기게 되었다. 그러면서 차츰차츰 하나씩 공부해나가기 시작했다. 시조를 하나하나씩 공부해 나가면서 처음에는 차근차근, 느릿느릿 번역해나갔다. 처음에는 너무 어렵고 힘이 든다는 생각이 들었다. 하지만 계속 해나가면서 힘이 붙기 시작했다. 거기에 자연스럽게 나는 고전문학에 대해 관심을 가지게 되었다. 거리감 느껴졌던 고전문학이 가깝게 느껴지게 된 것이다. 고전문학이 그저 알아보기 힘든 난해한 언어가 아니라 나에게 있어 특별한 의미를 지니게 되었다. 특히 시조에 대해서 '이건 내 것이다' 라는 애정이 생겼는데, 아무 관계도 아니던 고전문학과 나의 사이가 이제는 너무나 가까워지게 된 것 같다.

사실 고전문학을 좋아하게 되어서 고전문학 여행을 떠났다. 호남지방으로 여행을 가게 되었는데, 내가 자진해서 가족들에게 고전문학을 테마로 삼자고 한 것이다. 그런데 만약 여행을 가기 전 시조를 번역한 경험이 없었다면 여행은 그저 호남지방의 경치 좋은 곳을 구경하는 것에 그쳤을 것이다. 하지만 시조번역을 통해 고전문학이라는 것이 나에게 있어 정말 큰 의미를 지니게 되었기 때문에 여행에 별로 관심이 없던 내가 그렇게 능동적으로 참여할 수 있었던 것이다. 사실 나는 평소에 여행이라는 것 자체에 별로 관심이 없고 간다고 해도 부모님의 뜻에 따라 수동적으로 행동했었는데, 이 여행에서는 여행계획 등 모든 과정에서 즐거웠고

나 자신이 능동적이었다고 말할 수 있다. 고전문학 여헝은 고전시가의 향취를 직접 느낄 수 있다는 점에서 너무 좋았다.

고전문학이 한 지문 이상 출제되는 수능 시험을 치르게 될 수험생으로서도 이번 시조번역은 너무나 도움이 되었다. 고전문학을 잘 못 읽어내 허둥지둥 대던 내가 번역 후에는 여유롭게 읽고 문제를 풀어낼 수 있게 된 것이다. 단지 읽어내는 것에서만 도움이 된 것은 아니다. 시조를 공부하면서 옛 사람들의 세계관을 공부하고, 옛 사람들의 내면을 공부함으로써 작품을 더 깊게 이해할 수 있게 된 것이다.

세계적으로 유명한 일본의 하이쿠와는 달리 우리나라의 시조는 위기에 놓여있다. 나 역시 예전에는 시조에 관심을 가지지 않음으로써 그러한 위기에 기여한 한 사람이었지만 이제는 반대편에 서게 되었다. 시조번역을 하면서 관심을 가지게 되었고, 지금은 나 역시 우리 아름다운 시조의 보존 및 보급에 기여할 수 있는 사람이 되고 싶다.

시조번역 과정에서 외국인에게 의견을 묻곤 했다. 영어로 번역한 우리 시조를 통해 세계인과의 소통이 가능했던 것이다. 시조를 통해 우리가 느끼는 느낌을 다른 언어를 사용하는 사람에게 전할 수 있다는 것이 너무 신기했다. 언어가 이렇게 소중한 것이구나라고 새삼스레 느끼게 되었다. 언어에 대한 관심 또한 자라게 된 것이다.

선생님과의 또 다른 작업을 통해 앞으로도 우리나라 문학의 세계로의 진출에 기여하고 싶다.

Endnotes

[i] 'Neem' means lover.

[ii] the 'shool' here seems to be what Coreans have called 'mark-gerl-lee'. It is a traditional drink brewed from rice, now becoming very popular in Japan by the name, "mak-kol-li".

[iii] He is considered to be the number one scholar of Manners and Rituals during Chosun dynasty. After he died, his students basically ruled the country, except only for some period of time, until Chosun fell to the Japanese at the early 20th Century. The famous Yoon Sern-do was their political opponent, which explains why he had to spend most of his life in exile. .

[iv] 'Boong-marng' is the famous public tomb site in China

[v] He tried to protect the Boy King Darn-jong, only to fail, himself getting killed by the Boy King's uncle, King Sejo.

[vi] There is 'Narm Yi' island in Corea(http://www.namisum.com), named after this unfortunate young General. He was slandered to death at a young age of 27. The island was his private property and also the place he was exiled to before death. He was son of Yi Barng-wern's(His Shijo is on the page 147) daughter. The island is now a famous resort located in the North-East of Seoul. He wrote a poem in Chinese script, declaring that he would have to pacify the nation before he reaches 20 years old to be called a Real Man by the posterity. His political opponents, corrected 'to pacify' into 'to obtain', thus accusing him of planning a treason.

[vii] This Shijo heavily uses Chinese characters. The boy king is the grandson of the great king Se-jong, who invented the Corean alphabet. As it was right after the invention, it might not have been popular among the high grade officials and the privileged class.

[viii] He is believed to have been the teacher and lover of Hwarng Jin-yi, the top Shijo poetess.

[ix] The writer of this Shijo is a patriot during Bayk--je dynasty. He attempted to save his country, only to get killed by his own King. As it

was long before the Koryo dynasty when Shijo started, this verse is believed to have been attributed to him by posterity.

[x] She seems to have been a kisayng, geisha in Japanese.

[xi] This Shijo is a message that they should not be fighting each other. During the Chosun dynasty, the political battle was so severe that killing each other was a fairly common phenomenon.

[xii] Reading this Shijo, one would wonder what his achievement was. He is considered 'the top brush writer of Chinese letters in cursory style' of whole Chosun dynasty. His mother, a commoner, married to a high class official, killed herself to let his son rise to higher class. People must have asked him, "What is the good way to accomplish such a good writing style?"

[xiii] The Boy King Darn-jong was enthroned at the age of 12, dethroned at 15 by his uncle and killed at 17. When the Coup d'Etat broke out, the writer of this Shijo was in charge of the mission of taking the Boy King away from the court to the place of exile. This Shijo seems to be written on his way back from the mission. This year, on April, in the place of Cheong-ryeong-po, Kang-won Province, where the Boy King was exiled, marks the 44th annual 'Darn-jong cultural festival'.

[xiv] A popular song during the Japanese colonial period in the early 20th century, "Old castle" here refers to the capital of Koryo dynasty.

[xv] There is something about this writer. This writer's language style is so majestic that from his three Shijo extant, Coreans feel his charisma. Actually, it is said that even the king, only listening to his footsteps, changed himself right.

[xvi] Here, the Grand Palace refers to the palace site of Koryo dynasty. Some Shijo related books mistake it for "A grand pavilion". The original meaning of the so called "marn-werl-day" is the site of the capital city of Koryo, not some kind of constructional structure.

[xvii] He was the first grandson of king Sejo, so was entitled to the throne, but he lost it, because his brother's father-in-law, Harn Myerng-hoy was the man in power. As an older brother of then King, he may have felt the threat of assassination every single day of his life. Letting go of any kind of desire may have been the knowhow of his survival. This Shijo, though

a translation of a Chinese poem, was literally his own life.

[xviii] Kye'rarng is the same person as Yi May-charng (1513 ~ 1550)

[xix] The writer, hearing that the King surrendered to then, Ch'ing China, was on his way to the island Jeju to be a complete hermit, when he stopped by at this Bo-gil-do('do' means island). He was so fascinated by the beauty of it as to settle down there. He is believed, being rich, to have written songs and let dancers dance to his songs. But I personally visited the place and thought that he must have been extremely lonely, many times exiled out of the court, without close friends nearby. We may well believe that in this Five Friends Song, he is pleading his loneliness. The island, only because he lived there, now gathers tourists.

[xx] The writer was one of the six faithful servants who unsuccessfully campaigned to restore the Boy King Darn-jong to the throne. The six servants suffered severe torture to death.

[xxi] There is a park dedicated to her poetry, the May-charng park in Buan, her hometown in Jeonbuk province.

[xxii] 'ker-moon-go' is a stringed musical instrument, popular mainly among the literati.

[xxiii] The man failed to meet the true owner of his jade, so ended up crying in Mt. Hyerng in China.

[xxiv] "Marnsoo" means ten thousand years of life.

[xxv] The story has it that she once tore her clothes when a drunken man grabbed it, to keep her purity.

[xxvi] Many Shijo related books often mislead that May-hwar is plum and that it is the same with the family name 'Yi'. Though plum is the family name Yi, it is not May-hwar. Plum and mayhwar are totally different.

[xxvii] 'Kyu'jay' refers to 歐陽玄(1273 ~ 1357), a Chinese scholar who was the teacher of Yi Sayk.

[xxviii] [Someone's clothes being passed on] means that the clothes owner's teachings or literature are passed on for posterity. He is, maybe

arguably, considered to be the number one Chinese script poetry writer in whole Corea. He is credited to one Shijo. Today, we see his clothes are being passed on.

[xxix] One of the writer's descendants is General Yi Yeo-song(李如松) who, about 300 years later, came over as the Chinese 50,000 men strong Relief Army Commander to assist Chosun when the Japanese invaded in 1592.

[xxx] This Shijo blames Sheen Don, the reformist monk during late Koryo dynasty, who once wielded almighty power but later was taken down by King Kongmin who put him in power.

[xxxi] 'freeze' means literally freeze, but it also means to make love.

[xxxii] 'Aprok' river refers to The Yalu river

[xxxiii] The author was the architect of the new dynasty that toppled the Koryo dynasty. He was killed my Yi Barng-wern who killed Jerng Mong-joo.

[xxxiv] The sun refers to the king.

[xxxv] Together with Yarng Sar-ern, he was one of the top three brush writer during Chosun dynansty.

[xxxvi] 'Serl-do' was the famous poetess in T'ang China, so this was the highest compliment for her writing.

[xxxvii] In the original, the last segment in the second Line is an example of a sophisticated enjambment. It can be understood eithr as a part of the second Line or of the next Line or both.

[xxxviii] 'Yibool' is the bed cover that Coreans use.

[xxxix] This is not Shijo. It is longer version of the poet's one-Lined Shijo.

[xl] This one was not intended as a Shijo but the format is exactly a Shijo.

[xli] 'arjirarng'yi' is spring haze.

Index

Index of Old Shijo by the Title or the First line

Index of Modern Verses | Page

Index of Old Shijo by the Title or the First line

Shijo

Truly Corean Poetry Cadence Rhymed

저자 이경훈 김온승 박재우 이정은 한재은

초판 인쇄 2010년 8월 23일
초판 발행 2010년 8월 31일

발행처 도서출판 무송
발행인 권미순
등록번호 제2-1902호 (301-1995-008)
서울시 중구 인현동2가 169-1
전화 (02) 2274-0390

편집위원 이경훈 김온승 박재우 이정은 한재은
이메일 taran707@gmail.com

ISBN 978-89-962245-2-5 03810
값 15,000원

* 저자와의 협의에 의해 인지 생략함.